# MORE THAN JUST SKELETONS

In Pursuit of the Past

Jean Hendy-Harris

Copyright 2018 Jean Hendy-Harris

Other titles

*Chalk Pits and Cherry Stones*
*Eight Ten to Charing Cross*
*In Disgrace with Fortune*

ISBN-13: 978-1983555046
ISBN-10: 1983555045

*Non-fiction: memoir, 1950s London, poverty, family life*

An assembly of reminiscences to mark the life of my brother Bernard John Hendy who died in April 2016

# Contents

The Best and the Worst of Brothers ........................ 1
More than Just Skeletons ........................ 8
Ghosts of Christmas Past ........................ 16
Pride in Progeny ........................ 27
An Unanticipated Tea Party ........................ 33
When A Tiger Ate an Usherette Called Iris ........... 38
Adjusting What the Doctor Ordered ........................ 45
A Navigation of Northfleet High Street ................. 51
Getting To Know the Neighbours ........................ 61
Among Our Souvenirs ........................ 67
The Sad Passing of Playing With Fire ................... 73
Black Hands & Smoky Tea ........................ 80
Food, Glorious Food of the Forties & Fifties ........ 87
One of Them There Aphrodites ........................ 98
The House By The Station ........................ 109
Long Gone Pub Sounds ........................ 119
Remembering to Hate the Greeks ........................ 124
The Better People of Darnley Road ........................ 133
Walking Back From Gravesend ........................ 143
One or Two Canine Capers ........................ 150
What We Read Then ........................ 158
The Silver Lurex Jacket ........................ 163
The Vacuum Cleaner ........................ 170
A Constant Approach To Matrimony ........................ 173
The Blissful Burgeoning of Bathrooms ........................ 179
The Houses of Robinia Avenue ........................ 184
The Robin Hood of Wrotham Hill ........................ 190
Family Facts & Fantasies ........................ 198
First and Last Loves ........................ 207
About the Author ........................ 212

# The Best and the Worst of Brothers

The last time our immediate family could be found together was in Edinburgh in early June 2016, all five of us to attend a memorial service for my brother. His death had come without warning, out of the blue two months previously, whilst holidaying in Africa. It was said to have been the result of a sudden heart attack, the details of which we hoped soon to become acquainted with, but nothing was certain.

And so we stood, a little group thrown unexpectedly together in the foyer of a hotel in the Grassmarket, the historic centre of the magnificent Scottish city. Each of us now slightly discomfited by the abruptness of our assembly, searching for an innocuous topic on which to make initial casual comment and quickly seizing upon that which was the focus of our meeting, the death of Bernard John Hendy.

My own thoughts were on his birth in 1947, two months before my seventh birthday, when I would so very much have preferred to have had a sister. Then on his baptism that had caused such discord between my parents because at my mother's insistence it had not taken place in the Catholic Church on The Hill but at alien and Anglican St Mark's at Rosherville. Then as if this wasn't bad enough for my devout father, the last minute change of name. My new brother was supposed to be Bernard Joseph but because my mother harboured an aversion to certain names, she deftly substituted John at the very last second of the eleventh hour in a manner so unexpected that even the vicar, holding the infant above the baptismal font, looked startled. In exactly the same way she had seven years previously ensured that I became Jean rather than Bernadette. But now our family group did not speak of matters concerning the beginnings of life such as births and baptisms but of matters concerning the end.

A sudden death is hard to comprehend. An ending that comes out of the blue so disquieting that family, left emotionally stranded, find the circumstances almost impossible to internalise. So it had been with my brother who had so very recently enumerated to me the struggles he was having with his life and, fired with enthusiasm and inspired by an important new passion, the major changes he was intending to make. I listened, as an older sister is wont to do, and then being disturbed by the story, failed to give him the support he asked for. He told me that all he wanted was somebody to be on his side and I hesitated and shrugged because we both knew that somebody should be me. But I sent support scurrying in a different direction, feeling virtuous not because I wholly disapproved of all the preposterous plans that he proposed but because of the ripples of chaos he might create. The conversation had taken place a disturbingly short time ago and now we stood in the tall, forbidding Grassmarket building debating the impending memorial service to mark his death, a commemoration that had taken rather too long to organise. My prime emotion on that Edinburgh afternoon was a slowly evolving anger and I wondered if it would completely overwhelm me before I fully understood why I had abandoned him when he most needed me.

Now, he and I had simply run out of time for the accommodation of the plans we had made together. The book about our childhood would never now be written. No time was left for recording of reminiscences and ruminating on the past because as he once pointed out to me himself, memories aside, all that remained of our shared past were incidental box Brownie photographs, little black and white snaps taken in back gardens and on bomb sites.

I was supermarket shopping when he died. At an ungodly hour on account of an adjustment in the summer-winter clock I hovered over frozen peas and spinach, deliberated on their individual merits and compared prices. In the very last seconds of his earthly life I was very possibly queuing at the check-out counter, impatiently behind the Indian corner-dairy owners who always shop at hours unearthly despite summer-winter time variations. The news that his life had ended came an hour or so later by email from his son and left me in total disbelief because how could it possibly be that someone so charming and charismatic should simply vanish into the ether? We were brought up as Roman Catholics so surely his existence must not simply end just like that? After all, he was once an altar boy so didn't that count for something?

He and I had been raised in abject poverty, the kind of miserable and wretched neediness that doesn't exist anymore except in the underclasses of developing countries. We inhabited a world that makes Coronation Street look decidedly middle class. With the death of our father at the unseemly age of forty-one the privation and distress went to an entirely new level as our poorly-educated and well-meaning mother went on to do the best she could for us under very difficult circumstances. We lived in an area of largely industrialised Thameside where we were surrounded by the Decent Poor. We featured at the very bottom of the social heap because there were hints of Diddicai or Pikey family roots and the Decent Poor looked down on us. I can't say I blame them – when the neighbours were beginning to think about installing inside toilets with attached shower facilities, we were still hauling in the zinc bath from its place on the outside wall every Saturday night for the weekly bath. Bernard was convinced he was unpopular with other boys' families because he smelled bad and very possibly he was correct.

With our father safely and permanently absent I became his bullying older sister who had both loved him dearly and yet had wished him harm from the day of his first intrusion into my life. Left in charge of him whilst our mother worked cleaning other people's houses, I compelled him to eat slugs, chew marbles, beg in the street for pennies for a non-existent charity, and dress up as a girl called Wendy in a pink crepe-paper fairy costume I made specifically for the purpose. At the same time if any other child dared to criticize him I was ferocious in my defence and this merciless aggression on his behalf continued into his early teens when I once famously attacked three of his classmates who had unwisely risked upsetting him, sending the horrified trio bolting for cover. If necessary I would have killed for him.

He was a quiet and pensive small boy, unusually biddable so that it was generally impossible to know what he was really thinking. By the time he was four years old he had developed a fascination with and an impressively growing knowledge of backyard and hedgerow ornithology. The conversations he enjoyed most were those involving the conduct and actions of sparrows, starlings, blackbirds and finches. He told me that somewhat surprisingly it was our mother, and to some extent our grandmother who had inculcated this emergent interest that increased a thousand-fold over years until it became an all-consuming passion. By the time he was a young adult he had turned most of his attention to birds of prey, the magnificence of which regularly moved him to tears. It was this passion for bird life that from time to time dictated that I should also become involved, albeit unwillingly, and detailed to care for those rescued whilst he, accompanied by wife and small child, headed North to check on the well-being of others. And so I found myself nervously in charge of barn owls needing to be fed live mice and on one occasion a kestrel demanding a diet of voles and baby rabbits that I must somehow procure.

At the same time and perhaps oddly, Bernard had a chequered and volatile early life, frequent brushes with The Law and a tendency to stray far from the truth. He was a husband and father by the time he was eighteen and there were times when he could have done much better in both those roles, a fact of which he was painfully aware. During our last meeting he had impressed upon me, not for the first time, that he bitterly regretted being a far from ideal father during the earliest years of his only child's life. And now he desperately wanted to make up for those inadequacies with both love and with money and ensure that his now adult son would never be in need as he and I had been just one short generation previously.

We shared the same compulsion as we grew older. An uncontrollable urge that developed out of our joint inability to accept the reality of a vastly underprivileged start in life. It took the form of one invented substitute family after another, each more implausible than the last. This habit probably got my brother into more tight spots than it got me. Somehow I managed to see warning lights and extricate myself from trouble long before he did.

Bernard's second wife became for thirty years probably the most stable influence in his life. With her he was rapidly able to progress some of his dreams and become the person he really wanted to be. It was in some degree due to luck but also to her hard work and diligence that they together made a great deal of money and his long obsession with the Scottish Highlands was realised when he bought a Victorian mansion at Cape Wrath and turned it into a family home complete with enough power-showered bathrooms to utterly astound our former neighbours. His proximity to Britain's largest bird of prey, the Golden Eagle, was also of course a constant source of elation to him.

The marriage was a successful one for many years, perhaps because for Bernard it rapidly became based upon anxiety. A very tight ship was being run and there seemed no opportunity for the infidelities that had permeated his first marriage. He wisely adhered closely to the new rules and on this basis the marital bonds remained intact for a long time but not of course for all time and when the ties began to loosen our maternal grandmother would have undoubtedly noted that the proverbial apple had not fallen far from the tree.

He was immensely gratified to have become rich although money changed his basic personality very little. It was true he could now buy whatever he wished – and he did so, but essentially he remained the same. Without money he had always been unerringly generous and with money he simply became more so. And despite the unexpected hitches that often plague the lives of the newly rich he remained the captivating and magnetic individual he had always been, who could entertain with stories, many of which were quite untrue, for hour upon hour. He was always the best and the worst of brothers and at all times the brother who could not be entirely trusted because what he said might be true and equally well might not. He definitely knew I dearly loved him but he died without knowing how enormously proud of him I was, simply because I failed to tell him this. Later of course I wished I had voiced the details of my pride in his extraordinary knowledge, his unfailing kindness and humanity, and the way in which he could draw people to him so that their greatest wish was to gain his friendship.

Essentially life is short and when Death reaches out the separation and the silence seem so complete that we can never make too much of the ties and relationships we have with the living. With that sentiment in mind, this book is a somewhat fragmented memoir of our lives as we grew up together in the 1940s and 50s. It is perhaps the book we were planning to write together.

## More than Just Skeletons

One way and another Bernard had over the years done a great deal of research into the roots and background of both our mother's family, the Constants and our father's, the Hendys. In the first place his interest had been primarily in the latter as he tried to edge a little closer to the man who had so abruptly disappeared from his life that never-to-be-forgotten Christmastime when he was four years old. I had initially found this determination to uncover and verify facts rather less absorbing than he did and shuddered a little when he revealed one distasteful episode after another in the lives of our antecedents.

With enormous determination and effort he managed to trace The Hendy Family back into the eighteenth century but of course his greatest interest was in those members who came immediately before us. He was impatient to discover the reasons behind our father's disturbed childhood, spent variously in the Workhouse and finally in the Children's Homes of Chatham. There had always been a great deal of secrecy around our paternal grandmother, Kate, and as children we learned not to ask too many questions about her. When I discussed her with my Waterdales cousins I was told she had ended up in prison for beating some of her children to death. I wondered how many and was glad that our father had not been one of them. My cousin Connie said that it was her opinion that he had hidden in a cupboard or the khazi or perhaps even climbed a tall tree so she couldn't get at him. Our mother remained tight-lipped on the subject and said the matter didn't concern me and anyway not to use that word khazi because it wasn't very nice.

Bernard discovered that there had been a complete absence of murders and instead an addiction to alcohol, theft and fighting in the streets. This behaviour resulted in a number of prison sentences and committals to Oakwood Hospital better known as Barming Heath Mental Asylum. Kate was once called The Most Neglectful Mother in Chatham. This title was awarded her on November 16th, 1913 shortly before she was sent down for the fifth time. Her two youngest children, baby Elizabeth Mary and four-year-old Bernard Joseph, our father, were then temporarily removed to the Chatham Workhouse and from there into the care of local Children's Homes. Her six older children were distributed among Hendy relatives dotted in and around the towns and villages of North Kent.

Our mother was enduringly critical of the Hendy Family, holding them collectively responsible for what she saw as my father's unnecessarily disrupted and unhappy childhood. She simply could not understand why the two youngest children were cast aside so ruthlessly. She even pointed the finger at his oldest sister, all of fifteen years old, whom she felt certain could have Pulled Her Finger Out and taken care of her younger siblings. After all, the young Constants had all taken care of each other hadn't they? And the drunkenness and deprivation that abounded in Maxim Road, Crayford at the time was no secret. Blood was thicker than water she thought or it should have been.

The lack of concern for the two youngest children did seem curious but later, in the light of more persistent research when it transpired that they had not been Hendys at all but the progeny of a male who stubbornly remained unknown to us, the reasoning became clearer. Bernard was dejected and said that for years he had believed he was a Hendy and now it appeared obvious this was not so it left him with a strange and disconnected feeling. When I stopped to give that statement some consideration I found I felt similarly because the familial ties with the Hendys of Waterdales, those with whom I had shared so much of my early childhood, were looser than I had believed them to be. Perhaps that explained the hatred I had always felt for cousin George, two years my senior, seething resentment that had eventually resulted in me pushing him out of an apple tree resulting in what I was later told was an injured spleen. My brother readily agreed that there had not been overly much feeling of Belonging to those Hendys that we had known. It was at that stage that he gladly turned his attention resolutely to research of the Constants of Crayford.

The Constants immediately emerged as a dysfunctional and disreputable lot but we knew that anyhow having lived cheek by jowl with them for so many years but Bernard's investigations revealed that their overall status in their early years was lower than either of us might have expected. Most major family events, including our mother's birth into a hop bin, appeared to have occurred in the open air, which my brother now assured me was a definite indication of low social rank. Most of her siblings were either conceived or brought forth amid cereal crops or long grass and our grandfather expired among wet fish. Our mother was invariably vague when asked questions about the family origins and this indefinite attitude to enquiry seemed to be a characteristic that was inherited and over which she had little control. Perhaps it had originated in Ireland, in County Galway and was brought into England by our Great Grandmother whose firstborn, our Grandmother Margaret, usually referred to as Old Nan, continued the tradition of ambiguity and thus the seeds of the erosion of fact became well and truly sown.

Old Nan's marriage to Edgar Constant in the very first years of the twentieth century produced between thirteen and twenty-one children. True to form she was unclear with regard to the actual number and when questioned became distracted. When we tried to count them with the help of our many cousins we could only get to eleven or twelve even counting those who died as infants and so we came to the conclusion that there had possibly been a total of twenty-one pregnancies. What was clear, however, was that there was a great preponderance of girls and so we ended up with many aunts and only one uncle.

Our mother's upbringing rapidly conditioned her to the application of deceit as an essential tool of survival particularly where officialdom was concerned. Because casual agricultural work, especially hop picking, so preoccupied our grandmother it was impossible for the required registration of the births of her children within the six week time limit imposed at the time. As a consequence most of them had their birthdays adjusted and ended up with two or even three dates. One child failed to be registered at all and the demise of another at the age of eleven months resulted in the embarrassment of the death being registered prior to the birth.

The birth of our Uncle Edgar must have taken place at a completely inconvenient time as he was never actually registered at all and was forced to become a family secret and later a complete nonentity. In the eyes of both the State and the Law he simply did not exist. For the entire duration of his life Edgar was denied both the benefits and the protections of the welfare state. He was never required to attend school for instance which he felt gave him an enormous head start in the field of employment. And although he never enjoyed the blessings of Social Security or the NHS he claimed that not being called upon to participate in World War Two was a huge plus for which he remained eternally grateful. Thus, while others of his generation were giving their all in the struggle against National Socialism the youthful and energetic Edgar devoted himself both to the black market on the Home Front and to the comfort of the womenfolk of his fighting peers.

Our mother, Nellie, was the family's second born and followed her sister Margaret into a world of uncomplicated agricultural routine and they were soon joined by a new sibling each year. A number of the children died at birth or from childhood illnesses before their fifth birthday and two were inadvertently smothered when their drunken mother rolled over them whilst sleeping. Despite the attrition there were still a large number left to clothe and feed and life was not easy. The Constants had to earn a living and the harvesting of vegetables, fruit and hops was a lifeline for them. All else was secondary and certainly nothing as trivial as the registration of the birth of a child was allowed to get in the way of it. Owning no clock or calendar and being completely illiterate must have further hindered Old Nan and possibly there also existed a degree of genuine confusion. She conformed to a routine dictated by seasons and weather and most of all to the absolute necessity of earning money.

In general the Constants were a wild and unruly bunch, uncontaminated by the honesty and integrity of conventional society. Edgar their father showed a certain amount of entrepreneurial spirit and eventually worked his way up to becoming a prosperous wet fish merchant and haulier, and then worked his way all the way down again. It was rumoured that both alcohol and a touching faith in his fellow man combined to ruin him. Because of the family's long history of practised deceit it is hard to know the truth of the matter but it is certainly agreed that his ability to apply himself was not at fault. In the early days of the business, when the Depression was at its height, he would walk from Crayford to Billingsgate, arriving at first light to buy fish. He would then push an old pram full of fish back to Crayford where it was hawked around the new Council Estates. His enterprise was rewarded when the pram became a barrow, then a cart and later several carts and a lorry. He was a man who displayed undoubted potential.

On the other hand our grandmother was quite a different character. An alcoholic all her life she would from time to time claim teetotalism and even maintained this on her death bed despite the evidence of empty bottles beneath it. Unlike Edgar drink made her spiteful and vindictive. She lied to get money for alcohol, lied to explain the effects it brought upon herself and the family finances and lied to avoid accepting responsibility for her actions. When cornered she would place the blame upon others, even her own children, and she was more than capable of framing others and bullying her daughters with threats and violence into supporting her various deceits.

Nevertheless, despite her fierce temper tantrums and her frightening excesses, her children appeared to adore her and her misuse of them served only to fire their competition for her love and affection. She utilised their love to her own ends, expertly setting one against the other to protect herself introducing them all into the use of deception on a grand scale – against their father, their neighbours and each other until it became first nature to them all. Under her guidance they became schooled and practised in the art of obfuscation, honing their abilities to cloud any issue with a veritable shoal of red herrings until they were each a match for anyone in any situation. Within this situation our mother survived and thrived and rose to dominance. That we never enticed her to confirm precise details of the family history when we asked was merely a measure of our own naïve expectations

In his ongoing pursuit of truth my brother came across a disturbing number of predecessors with names like Boswell, Lee and Mayhew and whose professions were described as Horse Dealer, throwing some light at least upon the occasional finger pointing and whispers that we both well recalled from the past. And alongside he also discovered relatives any one of us could be proud of and as unlike Grandmothers Margaret Constant and Kate Hendy as it was possible to be. One such was Nelson James Constant who joined the Royal Artillery and served in India then in the Tower of London upon his return to England where his son, another Nelson James, was baptised in the Tower Chapel. Nelson James Constant lived a long life and became a Chelsea Pensioner, a distinction only bestowed upon those with exemplary records. He was buried with full military honours in Dartford proving to us both that the closet of family history contained more than just skeletons.

# Ghosts of Christmas Past

Like all children growing up immediately after World War Two, Christmas was for us less a time for being showered with expensive toys and more a time for church-going, early evening carol singing under lamp posts and partaking in seasonal treats such as mince pies, tangerines and candied pineapple. Despite the lack of material things, once the celebration of Guy Fawkes was over in early November, the entire child community of Northfleet turned with determination to the celebration of Christmas, greatly anticipating the apex of excitement that was soon to be theirs.

At St. Botolph's School on The Hill each year we were by mid-November deep in rehearsals for the Christmas Concert to which friends and parents were invited, and by the first week of December lessons were halted for thirty minutes each afternoon to allow us to make the two minute journey into the fourteenth century Church next door for Carol Practice. We always sang the same pieces at the end of year service - *Once in Royal David's City, The First Noel, It Came Upon The Midnight Clear, Hark The Herald Angels Sing, Oh Come All Ye Faithful, While Shepherds Watched Their Flocks By Night* and *Oh Little Town Of Bethlehem* and how easily the verses slip into memory even now.

The Christmas Concert I remember most vividly was the occasion when Betty Haddon sang *Alice Blue Gown*, Pearl Banfield and I dressed as Crinoline Ladies in crepe-paper costumes to dance a waltz and a contingent of the noisiest boys marched across the makeshift stage maintaining that there was A State Of War On The Nursery Floor whilst banging drums contrived from old biscuit tins. The excitement was intense. Then, quite suddenly school was finished and it was home to new Council Houses with fires in tiled surrounds for the luckiest among us and back to the tiny workmen's cottages where the heating was pre-Victorian for the rest of us.

Strangely we did not seem to notice how poor we were at Christmas, theoretically the time when it should have been most obvious, so powerful was the anticipated thrill of the impending celebration. On Christmas Eve the Salvation Army Band toured the streets for the final time and we donned coats and scarves and stood under the lamp on the corner of Springhead Road to listen before being ushered indoors once more for mince pies with cocoa for the children and a tot of cherry brandy for the grown-ups. Later my father would take me to Midnight Mass at the Roman Catholic Church where I happily shunted off my term-time Anglicanism and once again became a devout Catholic child both fascinated by the high drama of the Mass but bored at the same time because it went on far too long. He in his overcoat, demob suit and white silk scarf intent upon appraising any woman under fifty attending alone, was always in a good mood whilst maintaining an air of studied piety. My brother was considered too young to accompany us. Later he told me that he wished he had been included.

At this time of year both the Parish Priest, Father O'Connor, and a clutch of black-clad nuns would make a particular fuss of me and tell me I was a good child, hoping to lure me back to the school in Springhead Road where my brother was enrolled and would attend just as soon as he was four years old. On one occasion I was given Rosary Beads, ebony and silver that I kept for years. At the end of the mass there was generally a little Yuletide conversation between the attending parishioners during which my father was able to chat with the piano teacher from the top of Springhead Road and both the Murphy sisters who ran the Brownie pack next to the Library, hands nonchalantly in the pockets of his overcoat and laughing too loudly at their jokes. Once or twice I noted that he looked handsome and for a moment or two was proud of him.

Of course all children woke at dawn next day feverishly excited at the thought of what Father Christmas just might have brought with him and we were never let down because he always did bring something. One year it was a red plastic dolls' tea set from a stall at Gravesend Market, and another an exciting pile of second hand books including Rupert Bear and Toby Twirl Annuals. Breakfast on Christmas Day always began with mugs of sweet tea, laced with whiskey even for the children though I have absolutely no idea how and when this particular tradition began. Nevertheless I have followed it myself in the intervening years and have been oddly cheered to find that my own children do likewise though spread widely throughout the world.

There followed a range of festive snacks including the essential candied fruit, nuts and tangerines all so fundamentally part of Christmas that to this day the slightest hint of a tangerine or satsuma aroma instantly flings me back over decades to the late nineteen-forties.

Christmas Dinner was served fashionably late, certainly not before two in the afternoon and was generally one of our own hens, mashed and roast potatoes, sprouts and brown salty gravy followed by home-made Christmas Pudding and a white cornflour sauce heavily sweetened. My parents drank beer with this repast and my brother and I were deliriously excited to be given lemonade, exactly as if we were in the children's room at a local pub. We stayed up late and listened to the radio and on Boxing Day we went visiting either to Crayford to my mother's family or to Waterdales to my father's. Either way it was something I looked forward to because among my many cousins there was sure to be one who had been given a second-hand bike or even a passed-on china doll as Connie-on-my-father's-side was, one eventful year.

These largely happy Christmases were to change dramatically in 1951 and the years thereafter because that was the year our father died quite suddenly and inconveniently on the twelfth of December just a day or two after an afternoon of festive shopping in Gravesend. It was also the year when quality toys began to reappear in shops and there was to be a Meccano Set for my four-year-old brother which my father was looking forward to Helping Him With and an Art Compendium for me. These were absolute facts because he had been saving most judiciously since Guy Fawkes in order to ensure that an order could be safely placed with Father Christmas. Bernard did not quite appreciate what a Meccano Set actually was but the fact that his father was going to be fully involved in playing with it alongside him made him dizzy with excitement.

Despite the obvious drama that inexorably accompanies sudden death, for some reason we were not actually told although at eleven and a half years old I was aware that a momentous event had taken place. Quite unusually our father had visited the doctor in the days before his death. He was clearly unwell and his face had become far too yellow to be completely normal. At only four, Bernard was naturally less aware of these details and as time passed became even less cognizant of what had actually happened and the time sequence involved. Our missing father became a subject we did not discuss, most especially because at some stage I had been told that my brother was too little to really absorb such a critical happening. My mother was fearful as to how he would Take It. It then became as though he had never been and it was to be years before we mentioned his name one to another. Bernard was in his fifties when he told me of the concentrated research he had undertaken in order to try to find out just a little about Bernard Joseph Hendy, the father who seemed simply to evaporate one Christmastime along with the first insubstantial snowfall of the year. He had so very few real memories he said and he urged me to share my own with him. And so I was persuaded to return to a time I had tried very hard to forget and a sadness that was imprinted upon my heart.

It had been very early on a Tuesday morning when our mother ran to the corner shop as soon as they opened because therein was the nearest telephone. I hovered in the doorway of my parents' bedroom and studied my father feeling strangely anxious although he and I had failed to establish a close relationship since he came back from the war after an absence of more than five years. I would have been more than content for him to once again become the father who lived only in the photograph beside the wireless and to whom I blew perfunctory kisses on my way to bed. Now I felt uneasy as I noted the over-yellowness of his skin against the white pillow-slip, newly changed for the hopefully impending visit of the doctor. He opened too-yellow eyes momentarily and made some inconsequential comment about me not being late for school and that was the last time I saw him, those words concerning school were the last he was to speak to me. Two days later he would die in Gravesend Hospital and whilst he did so my brother and I were left at home in the care of our teenage cousin Margaret who gave us peppermints and played Ludo with us and allowed Bernard to cheat so that he won every game.

The day before his death, making tea for an aunt and a neighbour, my mother had appeared oddly self-assured, almost jaunty, setting milk and sugar on the kitchen table, counting out cups and making comment that Bern had been relieved to get into that hospital, really glad he'd not decided to simply Sleep It Off, whatever it was that was draining his strength, turning him yellow. Twice he'd said to her – 'It was the right decision to come here Nell!' And to think she'd been feeling uncomfortable about the doctor dropping them off there in his car. Driven them himself he had. It was good of him. Children were allowed to visit on Sundays. She was going to take the kids in, well Jean at least. Listening to this exchange I was reassured and hopeful he would be well again in time to slaughter the

Christmas Dinner hen. The killing was anything but pleasant but I was looking forward to helping with the plucking even though the feathers hovering about us in the scullery made me sneeze and cough.

The day he died was a Thursday but for some reason neither my brother nor I had been sent to school although both of us would have been happy to go. Bernard because it was his very first term at St Joseph's in Springhead Road and it was still a relatively novel experience. At playtime each day he would stand by the playground fence that adjoined the Old Green bomb site because sometimes if he was on two-to-ten shifts his father would walk over and talk to him through the fence and once he gave him a toffee. But that had been when he was still a New Boy of course, a reward for not crying. I would have willingly gone to school because of all the excitement of the end of year Concert festivities. This year I was to be an angel in a white crepe-paper costume that my mother had yet to make. I hoped my father's ill-timed illness would not get in the way of the costume making. Last year I had been Mary, mother of Baby Jesus in a Real Pageant and sat beneath the Lychgate of St Botolph's Church with my doll Susan being the baby. I had been specially chosen by the Bishop himself who said I had the face of an angel and although Old Nan said the evening was cold enough to Freeze the Balls off a Brass Monkey I hadn't noticed because my excitement was great.

During that afternoon of the many Ludo games in which Bernard was allowed to cheat, as shadows began to fall over the Old Green I clearly remember the taxi that brought the hospital visitors back from Gravesend, a black vehicle seeming oddly sinister in the half-light that spilled out its passengers onto the edge of the bomb site. My mother with bent head and weeping was supported between two aunts and barely able to walk down the garden path. It was clear that some unexpected or unwelcome event had taken place. Perhaps my father was no longer happy to be at the hospital and demanding to be allowed to return home.

Once inside, the aunts whispered a lot, fed my mother a white tablet and put her upstairs to bed where she continued to cry but more softly. Aunt Mag mouthed to Margaret a stage whisper to the effect that my father had Now Gone and Bernard overheard and wondered where he might have gone to. He asked me so I took him into the scullery and told him he would be back in a week or two but by then good sense was beginning to tell me that of course that wasn't so. Margaret cried almost as much as my mother and that was because she had loved my father very much, in fact much more than I had. For a while I went upstairs and lay alongside my mother and asked for reassurance that now he was in the hospital my father would get well again even though I knew that was not so. Through her tears she told me that of course he was going to get well again and I began to feel tightly knotted anger at the dishonesty.

I was embarrassed to go downstairs again because of the whisperings of truth that were not being extended to me but once my mother was sleeping I did so and by then it was completely dark. Margaret and I were sent out to fetch fish and chips for tea as a treat and once he heard this Bernard began to smile because he loved chips but I knew I was too angry to eat any. On the way I asked Margaret if my father was going to get well again and she began to cry all over again and told me that of course he would. I hated her then. My anger and resentment continued to grow over the following days when a funeral at which neither my brother nor I were present, must have taken place.

    There followed the strangely embarrassing situation of neighbours calling in giving gifts to my brother and myself, boxes of scented handkerchiefs, Mickey Mouse Soap and chocolates. None of this felt quite right and people were speaking far too quietly. A parent dying at Christmastime is distressing for everyone and the guidelines for how to best deal with it are sparse so little wonder that our mother dealt with the situation badly. Both Bernard and I went on to deal equally badly with each Christmas that followed, not only into our young adulthood but also into advancing age, each of us feeling the sharp pangs of remembered childhood misery as the festive seasons approached even though memory of that first pain was now almost completely lost . We strove to hide the uncomfortable memories under excessive and extravagant celebration and to a large extent we each succeeded. My mother managed less well and although every Christmas that followed featured half a bottle of cherry brandy to accompany the mince pies and a small bottle of whiskey for the early morning tea, they were by and large melancholy affairs. The Christmases I later structured in New Zealand, however, were Victorian in their magnificence and quite out of kilter with what was locally acceptable and left each of my three children with just a little longing for a more customary barbecue on the beach.

It was to be years before I would become aware that there had been a post-mortem on our father that revealed the condition that caused his death was acute hepatitis which in itself may or may not have been the result of an illness he had during the war, amoebic dysentery. This was the illness that had led to him needing an extended convalescence on a farm in Tunisia where he had become extremely popular with the family and where Little Andre, who may or may not have been our half - brother, was born. It was also many decades before I began to think about the significance of the two officials who visited our home at some stage following all the drama. Men in grey suits and raincoats who questioned my mother and took a great interest in the Anderson Shelter and the chemicals that had been used to clean and refurbish my father's motor bike. They gave particular attention to the bottles of Carbon Tetrachloride and took a number of things away with them and forgot to tell my mother they were sorry for her loss.

Later the motor bike was sold but because it was largely in pieces the fortunate and enthusiastic buyer didn't pay much. Nevertheless my mother was glad to see the back of it because she'd never felt safe on it or indeed its predecessor, the Ariel. The Ariel had been sold in 1949 and proudly replaced by the red and silver Harley-Davidson. The bike had been, of course, my father's pride and joy and stood in pride of place very close to my young brother who was also his pride and joy. Sadly, he was never able to get as much pleasure out of me, his overly critical and suspicious daughter who never quite forgave him for returning from World War Two in the first place to disrupt the uneventful but contented life my mother and I shared together. Even so his abrupt departure from our lives five years later left an emotional cavity that my mother found difficult to fill and although I had found his presence at times challenging, I began to find his absence even more so. My first emotion, however, when finally discovering that he was not ever coming back again, was one of relief and I fervently hoped that we would be able to return to that wartime life when it seemed to me we had no problems whatsoever.

    It would be true to say that when he shuffled off his mortal coil so precipitously that year when I was eleven and Bernard was four, Bernard Joseph Hendy deftly changed forever the way his children viewed the Festive Season, forcing us into a regular appraisal and examination of indeterminate Ghosts of Christmas Past every twelve months without fail.

# Pride in Progeny

It might have been the candid confession regarding the depth of his childhood despair over various aspects of his upbringing that caused first Bernard and then me to finally cast aside mistrust of each other and replace it with intense filial affection. It happened quite suddenly.

I was six and three quarters when he was born and from the moment of his entrance into the grimy Northfleet community I resented him with an astonishing level of bitterness. Those were the days when older female siblings were routinely placed in charge of the newest family members and it was clear that our family was not going to differ in this respect. By the time I had reached my seventh birthday I was Baby Minder in Chief, regularly directed to walking and pram rocking duties after school. Many of the older sisters around me seemed to enjoy the responsibility of these duties and in fact if you didn't have your own resident infant it was quite acceptable to borrow one from a neighbour. The most desirable were females dressed in pink especially those with cutting edge names like Cheryl-Anne or Sharon-Louise, names that might even be embroidered onto the huge fleecy pram pillows.

My father was delighted with his son and could love him in a way that he clearly found difficult with me. He was eager for him to grow bigger and stronger so that he could introduce him to all those things I found abhorrent such as funfairs and football matches and long walks on the Thameside marshes. It was this very marshland where as he grew older Bernard was to spend day after day in happy observation of Oystercatchers and Brent Geese and where he was to excitedly report to me just after his eleventh birthday that he had noticed Spotted Redshanks feeding with the Greenshanks. But then none of this was of the slightest interest to me because I was totally engrossed in the excitement of being a shorthand typist in the Music Industry. But in the summer of 1947 when Bernard was just a few months old my father's undisguised anticipation of the future father-son relationship filled me with a strange unease and perhaps it was then that I first began to nurture the idea of swapping our baby for a more acceptable sibling.

Brenda Stewart's mother had given birth to a baby a mere day or two after we took delivery of Bernard but hers was a girl called Judy. How I envied Brenda. If we had to have a baby at all then why couldn't it be a girl? In fact Brenda and I discussed this very situation fairly regularly as she was now detailed on similar after school pram duties to me. She even elaborated on the matter of her family's desire for a male child saying they were going to call him Richard if he had eventuated as hoped. I recall thinking idly that if fate bestowed our Bernard upon them it probably wouldn't be too much of an upheaval for him to have his name changed, Richard being a nice enough name and overall the loss of him wouldn't be the end of the world because we would still be able to see him from time to time.

I can't recall with any clarity when I first proposed the baby swap idea but within a day or two I do know that Brenda had enthusiastically agreed and the two sleeping infants were duly switched. I took the slumbering Judy home with me feeling satisfied and only a little bit nervous. Several hours passed before a furious Mrs Stewart turned up at our door angrily demanding the return of her Judy and darkly advising my shocked mother that there was something not quite right about me because I was certainly Old Enough to Know Better! When my father returned from work I was soundly thrashed for this misdemeanour, the first of many such beatings concerning wrongs done to my brother after which I would bear the bruises for a fortnight. I was also sent to bed at six pm without any tea for a week which I considered most unfair. I thought then, and even now, that the beating itself should have been punishment enough. However, it seemed unwise to attempt to debate this at the time and in those days harsh reprisals often followed quite minor misdeeds, so I lay in bed plotting revenge whilst other children played outside in the street and as it grew dark were called home one by one to their tea time jam sandwiches.

Bernard of course had been far too young for the day When He Was Swapped to have any effect upon his psyche although in more recent years he waxed lyrical and lengthily upon the distress caused when I did things like sabotaging the flight path of his yellow plastic helicopter. Being responsible for his arm being detached from its socket when he was two did not please him either. The latter was an event I only barely recall but one that hugely impacted upon him, presumably because it had been very painful.

On the surface he had not seemed to be a troublesome boy but he was one who became ever more delinquent with the passing years and most of his juvenile misdemeanours he managed to either get away with completely or somehow or other shift the blame from himself onto others. By the time he was nine years old he was a seasoned and accomplished liar and the impressive catalogue of his juvenile offending was later to astonish me.

It was to be years before I would uncover the truths of these transgressions, the various acts of thievery and violence and manipulation of the goodwill of both his circle of friends and family members. It was these latter lapses of accepted norms of behaviour that shocked me most; the stealing at the age of twelve of our mother's entire Christmas savings, carefully hidden in an old glove box at the top of her wardrobe and added to week by week, money accumulated in order that she could provide festive treats for him. The spur of the moment theft of two five pound notes from a visiting uncle's wallet trustingly left in the pocket of the jacket that Bernard helpfully hung on the pegs at the bottom of the stairs. The casual sale of my entire record collection to a second hand dealer in Gravesend, LPs and 78s I had optimistically purchased in the hope I would one day be in a position to afford the record player that should go with them. With the execution of these acts he deftly proved himself to be worthy of acceptance into any Diddicai family.

Somehow or other our mother managed to cover up a great deal of his behaviour, made excuses for him, extracted promises that it would never occur again and even explained the missing record collection by maintaining she had put it in an upstairs cupboard so it would be safe. However she failed miserably when he ran off with the week's takings from a local butcher's shop only two weeks after she had found him the job. He had no desire for a career in butchery it appeared but in any event this was a more serious incident that involved violence upon the unfortunate envoy on his way to the bank and eventually resulted in a court appearance. Before that took place, however, Bernard had arrived distressed and distraught on my doorstep in West London in search of protection. He had already purchased a tent and a pair of binoculars and thought he might hitchhike to Scotland and spend the rest of his life in search of Golden Eagles. He was just fifteen years old.

It has to be admitted that neither of us were the kind of progeny a parent could easily be proud of although had she lived long enough I think our mother would have eventually taken pride in Bernard. She would undoubtedly have been pleased by the fact that finally he became the kind of father that he had longed to have himself. She would have been astounded by his wealth and she would have been gratified by the depth of his love and concern for others. She would have more than willingly joined the constant Family Reunions he became fond of organising at Cape Wrath Lodge and taken her place as the Grand Matriarch, wearing her best dress and the crystal beads poor Fred, a long deceased fiancé, had bought for her. She would have taken great pleasure in the way others admired her now more-than-socially-acceptable son and how long and loud they laughed at his jokes and his stories. But she might also have felt more than a twinge of concern for the streak of gullibility that remained present to the end of his life, making it possible for him to, quite surprisingly, find himself among the deceived rather than the deceivers. It was astonishing how those closest to him could most effortlessly seem to betray him.

## An Unanticipated Tea Party

During the time when we were being given the attention and unexpected treats that people extend to suddenly bereaved children, we were invited to tea by my father's foreman from the Cement Works who had a family of two slightly hysterical girls called Brenda and Sylvia, and two foster sons called Kevin and David. They were what my mother called Good People and attended a Methodist Chapel regularly. We were excited and more than a little anxious. Being invited out to tea was not something we were accustomed to. Dressed in our best clothes, we walked the two miles from York Road and almost into Gravesend via Perry Street and I had to hold Bernard's hand all the way and remind him that he had to Behave. It was a bitterly cold January day but there was a cheerful fire in the foreman's living/dining room which was impressively quite separate from their kitchen. Theirs was an upper-working-class terraced house with a little front garden and a narrow entrance hall which at the time I considered to be luxury living. Just imagine coming home to a house with an entrance hall and thus not having to walk directly from the street into the front room! Furthermore I later discovered this lavish residence also had an inside toilet in a real bathroom where little pink fluffy towels were available if you happened to want to wash your hands. As I was not in the habit of washing my hands after visiting the toilet, no-one in our extended family thinking it was necessary, I did not use them but instead tried to imagine the indulgence of never having to don coat and scarf before traipsing forth into the backyard on winter nights.

There was a freshly ironed blue and white cloth on the table and it was set for six – the two excitable girls, their young foster brothers and we two. A plate of bread and butter was in the centre and beside it a little dish of strawberry jam with a spoon, another plate of assorted biscuits and pieces of homemade gingerbread and in the very middle of the table, in pride of place, six chocolate tea cakes wrapped in silver paper. I knew at once what they were because I had often longingly examined them in their tempting red and white boxes in Trokes' corner shop, and at the Co-op. My mother never bought them because they were, she said, much too pricey but occasionally opted instead for a more substantial Lyons Individual Fruit Pie which could be cut into sizeable portions, feed three and still be considered a Treat.

We sat at the table more than a little ill at ease because of our excitement. It was just like being in a Noel Streatfield story. Bernard was offered bread and butter with jam which he unhesitatingly turned down in favour of gingerbread and biscuits. I had read enough about this particular social situation to know we were meant to begin with the bread and butter option and so, glaring at him just a little, I did so, working my way methodically towards the gingerbread and biscuits and hoping to be seen as a role model. Bernard was asked if he would like another piece of gingerbread which he refused. Would he perhaps like a chocolate tea cake the hovering foreman's wife asked? He nodded enthusiastically and could scarcely get the silver paper off fast enough, then looked at the dainty morsel as if he could not believe his good fortune before beginning to slowly nibble around the edges. The rest of us began a stilted afternoon tea conversation about the latest Enid Blyton book that Brenda was reading, all the while taking glances at the miscreant in our midst. I was torn between fury towards my brother for letting me down on the very first occasion in my life I was invited out to tea, and anger at myself for not warning him in advance about the importance of social etiquette. Of all this my brother remained blissfully unaware.

One of the boys pointed out that it wasn't fair to get a chocolate tea cake without eating any bread and butter. He was quelled by a fierce look from his foster mother and in the interim Bernard's progress around the edges of the teacake had become rapid and he was already licking odd bits of chocolate from his fingers. 'That was very nice', he remarked conversationally and shook his head when offered biscuits or more gingerbread. Meanwhile even whilst engaging in conversation, all the host children except Kevin had demolished the required amount of bread and biscuits and were tucking into their own chocolate tea cake. I joined them. One solitary silver wrapped cake remained in the middle of the table, now eyed anxiously by Kevin. The host mother urged him to hurry up and began to take off her pinny and folding it, cheerfully asking if her two guests would like something more. I shook my head. Bernard was now sitting on both his hands, his cheeks slightly red, a smear of chocolate on his chin. He paused for an agonising two or three seconds and then to my extreme horror said loudly, nodding towards the centre of the table – 'I'd like that tea cake please'.

She gave it to him immediately whilst Kevin began a howl of protest about that particular tea cake definitely being his. He was ignored by Bernard who hastily ripped off the covering and began to cram it into his mouth before she could change her mind. Kevin threw himself on the floor and crawled under the table, continuing to cry loudly. David swung to and fro on his chair making baby noises. The two girls looked wide-eyed and shocked, mouths open. I wished a hole would appear in the Axminster carpet for me to disappear into. I had never in my eleven and a half years of life felt so utterly humiliated and let down – imagine having a brother who ate the last tea cake! What could possibly be worse? I decided that on the way home I would definitely not hold his hand.

I demanded an explanation of him before we reached the corner of Perry Street. Bernard unhesitatingly explained that he had wanted the second tea cake very much indeed. Through clenched teeth I snarled that it was obvious he wanted it but that eating the last teacake simply wasn't done and he wanted to know why not. I considered giving him some extended punishment but in the end thought better of it. Probably as he grew older and learned to read proper books with chapters, he would begin to understand the rather complex social rules pertaining to those who aspired to join the lower middle classes and thus be invited out to afternoon tea where exotic items like teacakes were served in the first place. It had begun to snow on the way back and when we got home there was a huge fire in our kitchen.

Our mother wanted to know if they'd given us a good tea. Bernard told her, 'Yes, it was good. They have different jam to us – it doesn't come in a jar – it comes in a dish…and they have chocolate teacakes in silver paper. I ate two of them and I kept the paper.'

The firelight danced against the walls making shadows jump as we watched him pull several wrinkled and creased pieces of red and silver paper from his pocket. He placed them gently on the edge of the kitchen table and began to examine them reverently, softly commenting that they were Really Very Beautiful. I was surprised to find my eyes filling suddenly with tears so I bolted upstairs before either of them noticed.

## When A Tiger Ate an Usherette Called Iris

People don't talk much about Going To The Pictures these days so maybe they simply don't go or more likely they have an up to date and conventional term for the pastime like Seeing a Movie. Back in those years that followed the war we definitely went to the Pictures and to do that we went to a Picture House. My own favourite Picture House was the Wardona in Northfleet though I visited the place fairly infrequently because my mother was sure I would Catch Things there. The things she most feared me catching were Nits and TB. She favoured the Majestic in Gravesend which was flashily decorated in red and gold. Old Nan, our maternal Grandmother who knew everything about the Pictures, said the Majestic had opened in 1931 and at the time had a café for patrons and four dressing rooms for the convenience of those appearing in Live Shows. I don't actually remember any Live Shows but I suppose there must have been some at one time. It was certainly a popular place in the late 1940s and early 1950s with long queues outside on some Saturday nights, depending upon what was showing of course. At popular times there was an organist called Reggie New and an usher who walked up and down the queue calling out, 'Seats in all places'. When I was very small I have a faint memory of us going to see Casablanca there which I found exceedingly boring . We also saw Bambi and Snow White which were both considerably less tedious even though the forest fire was alarming and the witch terrifying.

Of the four Gravesend cinemas my own preference was for the Regal. To be perfectly honest I was not keen on frequenting the Majestic by myself especially when attempting to get into an age restricted programme because the woman in the ticket office was particularly astute at querying if you were really fourteen or actually only twelve. If you were in fact only eleven that could be quite awkward despite the plush surroundings. The Regal was less lavish and had been designed by someone called Charles Lovell, opening as long ago as 1914. It had 750 seats in the auditorium and over 300 in the balcony as well as two boxes for the local elite. It had originally been called the Gem Picture Theatre but in 1934 it was taken over by Union Cinemas, spruced up and renamed the Regal. Old Nan clearly remembered the re-opening in May of that year because she and my grandfather had come all the way from Crayford to attend and catch a glimpse of not only Jessie Matthews but Doris and Elsie Waters also. It was clearly quite an occasion and after the excitement of rubbing shoulders with the stars they had treated themselves to a fish supper in the High Street before downing a number of Gin & Tonics at the Three Daws. This story, told a number of times as I was growing up, did not impress me at all because I had no idea who Jessie Matthews was and only a dim awareness of Elsie & Doris Waters who were to me, two very boring radio personalities who seemed to say things that amused my mother and most of the aunts.

The most noteworthy feature of the Regal as far as I was concerned was that the staff in the ticket office were generally not quite as fussy as those at the Majestic and because of this eleven and twelve year olds were privy to a wide and exciting range of restricted programmes that these days would not raise an eyebrow but at the time were considered pretty racy. Regal fussiness was more to do with allotting seating and the two usherettes were quite determined that anyone who looked under the age of fifteen must sit as far Down The Front as possible and preferably in the first two rows, in fact in the cheapest seats, tickets for which I seem to recall were a mere nine-pence. This was usually easily enforceable because child patrons generally had in fact purchased the cheapest seats and in any case in those days as a rule children did what adults told them to unless there was a fool-proof way of not doing so.

Despite our on-going poverty my mother was not in favour of the cheapest seats where Picture Houses were concerned because she had read somewhere that viewing from too close a proximity to the screen would inevitably lead to blindness in later life. She firmly believed that my Grandmother's cataracts were a consequence of this habit. Therefore although we were not as frequent cinema attenders as our neighbours, when we did go we always sat at the Back, in the Good Seats, sometimes paying as much as one and nine-pence at a matinee performance. So when my brother and I were sent off on a Saturday afternoon in March 1953 to see The Greatest Show On Earth starring the dashing and handsome Cornell Wilde with whom I had fallen passionately in love, although I was not quite thirteen and Bernard only six years old we were given the exact money and told to only buy Best Seats. I importantly joined the ticket office queue and duly purchased two one and nine-penny tickets. It was quite a surprise therefore when presenting them to the bored afternoon shift usherette to be ordered with a simple flash of her torch to 'Go down the front'. I carefully held the tickets up again for inspection and said firmly, 'I've paid for back row tickets – one and ninepence each!' Looking a little impatient and raising her voice she flashed the all-important torch down the aisle. 'All children down the front,' she said abruptly and quelling my next protest before I could actually utter it she added, 'And no further lip from you if you don't mind.'

In fact I did mind because I had been about to enlighten her about the blindness that could eventuate from sitting too close to the screen. I minded very much and had begun to feel just a little bit fearful of a possible confrontation but also highly indignant. Bernard tugged at my hand anxiously and looked as if he was about to cry. 'Let's do what she says,' he urged. But I had already decided to ignore her because Right was on my side and so I began to drag him into one of the back row seats whereupon she took his other arm and started to propel him towards the front of the auditorium with her torch prodding into his back every step or two. Infuriatingly he obediently went ahead of her more intent upon not missing the beginning of the afternoon programme than the Rights and Wrongs of the situation. The Pathe News had in fact started and was showing dramatic footage of the devastating recent tidal surge that had even affected people we knew of in Northfleet and killed hundreds that we didn't know at all. But I had already begun to feel the stirrings of fury that in subsequent years would become all too familiar a sensation when face to face with

Injustice and Discrimination. Rushing ahead of the now huge arc of her torch I pulled him back, holding his upper arm firmly with one hand and the one and ninepenny tickets now becoming creased and sweaty with the other. The all-powerful Usherette had stopped sounding bored and was repeating loudly that all children must sit in the front two rows and furthermore she was in no mood for Backchat.

But on the way into the auditorium I had idly noticed a door that said Manager's Office. Managers I knew had power and sorted out problems. 'I'm going to see the Manager,' I said firmly, 'Because you shouldn't be making us sit in cheap seats when we've got tickets for dear seats.' She shrugged but just a little diffidently and advised me to Suit Myself but that no rules would be bent on my account and say-so, she could guarantee that.

Bernard had begun to cry properly now, big tears rolling down his cheeks and his shoulders shaking. 'I just want to see the circus people,' he sobbed. I told him he would definitely see the circus people because the Manager would sort out the problem and as I spoke I visualised a performing tiger tearing out the throat of the odious woman with the torch, forcing her to drop it in the aisle as she screamed in anguish, vainly trying to fend off the animal but not before it crunched her vocal chords and turned its attention to the wrenching of her right arm from her shoulder. This particular circus scene was so very pleasing that I pictured it all over again before plucking up the necessary courage to knock on the door that said Manager's Office.

I banged on the door as loudly as I could but nothing happened until I knocked for the third time. He was short and plump and looked ill-tempered; patches of underarm sweat were evident on his otherwise whiter than white shirt. He had blue braces and a jacket draped over the chair-back beside him in the tiny space. 'What do you want?' he asked irritably, glancing at Bernard whose nose was now running because of all the tears.

Battling the inner turmoil I was feeling I explained the problem as calmly as was possible and also elaborated on the reasons why – the danger of blindness in later life emanating from the first rows of the stalls. I added that my grandmother's eyes had suffered on account of the Front Stalls habit. I showed him the creased and now very damp tickets which he smoothed on his blotter, nodding as he did so, 'Yes these are back stalls all right' he said. Still looking exasperated he led the way back into the auditorium which was now nicely filling and called to the abhorrent usherette, 'Iris – these patrons have the correct ticketing for back seating.' She shrugged again and told him that only a moment ago the kiddies had seemed to have lost their tickets and if only she had seen them there wouldn't have been a problem in the first place.

'She's a liar,' I said and turned to Bernard for support but he was still weeping though more quietly now. He was in no state to support me. The Manager sat us in the back row just as the last Pathe Gazette item finished. A moment or two later he returned with a packet of Polo Mints which he handed to Bernard who stopped crying at once.

Despite the undoubted attractions of Cornell Wilde, Trapeze Artist, I didn't feel entirely normal for at least half an hour, endlessly reliving the bloody demise of the much-despised Iris, she whom the circus tiger pinned to the sloping aisle of the Regal Cinema and then consumed so completely that all that was left of her by intermission was the abandoned torch still shining its arc towards the screen. Beside me my brother now cheerfully munched on Polo Mints and sniffed only very occasionally.

As we waited for the bus home he said, sounding suddenly very grown up, 'It's worth complaining isn't it Jean?' I nodded and tried to appear sophisticated, still feeling edgy and ill at ease about what had happened. In an offhand voice I advised him to always appeal to the Manager if a problem should emerge. I imagined that those in the bus queue admiringly applauded this most mature attitude.

Decades later, on a visit back to Gravesend after the Regal had become first a Bingo Hall and then the United Church of the Kingdom of God, I was abruptly reminded of that afternoon when I had been ardently in love with Cornell Wilde and when a tiger ate an usherette called Iris.

## Adjusting What the Doctor Ordered

Our doctor was always Dr Outred of De Warren House on the London Road. My mother maintained he was definitely the best doctor in the area, much better than Dr Crawford on The Hill and that was because he was a surgeon as well as being an ordinary run-of-the-mill doctor and that signalled being Extra Special! That's not to say that we were in the habit of consulting him all that frequently because before 1947 and something called The National Health Act it cost half a crown a visit and that meant the benefits of each possible consultation had to be weighed carefully in advance. It was definitely not something to be rushed into. So when my mother had some kind of abscess in her throat during the winter of 1942 she put up with it for several days before consulting Dr Outred who apparently swiftly lanced it giving her a story to dine out on for several years to come, had she been in the habit of dining out which of course she was not. The lancing, she informed anyone who would listen, was on account of him being a Surgeon and possessed of a certain amount of skill with several varieties of blade. Subsequent to the drama of the lancing she felt so much better that her faith in him increased mightily.

He then had the foresight to add to his overall mystique by saving my life when I was four years old and suffering from Pneumonia. I should explain that it was not even Ordinary Pneumonia either, but the Double variety and although I have never been entirely clear about what separates the Ordinary from the Double, the dramatic event itself I actually remember with reasonable clarity. I had been put to bed in my pink and cosy winceyette nightgown well wrapped in blankets with the added precaution of a roaring fire in my bedroom. Feeling decidedly unwell I idly observed the giant sized wooden Dutch Dolls that now entered the room carrying a trestle table which they set up at the bottom of my bed before calmly and methodically consuming the contents of a wicker hamper. I watched in fascination as they munched their way through a number of pink iced cakes decorated with cherries, aware that had I been feeling just a little better I might well have been envious. My mother hovered over me with hot lemon juice laced with honey and at some stage my condition was deemed to be such that Old Mr Bassent from next door went to call for the doctor to come which perhaps meant crossing the road to the corner shop to use the telephone. By the time he arrived I was sitting on the curtain rail above my own bed, alongside a number of hunched and ugly shiny bronze goblin-like creatures that I remember thinking looked about the size of those strange individuals who lived inside the wireless in the kitchen, those who read the news and told jokes that made people laugh a lot. Perhaps they were indeed from the wireless because it was feasible now I had become much smaller that I would soon be going to live with them on the shelf in the corner of the kitchen next to the scullery door. I hoped I would be able to still see my mother from inside the wireless. It was possible that the front panel also contained a window big enough for those inside to observe what was going on in the parallel world of full-size humankind. I certainly hoped so.

And while these jumbled thoughts occupied me I calmly witnessed Special Dr Outred who was also a Surgeon peeling the layers of clothing from me and looking disapprovingly at the banked-up fire before striding to the window beneath me and to my mother's horror opening it wide. Even the goblin people muttered to each other when that happened. Then I was given a most Magical injection of what was described to the neighbours the following day as a Wonder Drug. My life had been saved and I then recovered in a most remarkable manner.

Later, when Bernard was two or three years old his life was also very nearly saved when that same Doctor cleverly diagnosed the nasty condition to do with an infection in the bones adjacent to his right ear before sending him into Joyce Green Hospital at Dartford for several weeks. Bernard did not think much of the experience and retained a fear of hospitals for the rest of his life.

Nevertheless it's easy to see why my mother felt she had a lot to thank Dr Outred for although later when he killed my father she naturally enough changed her mind and never felt quite the same about him again. To be completely fair it was Old Nan who first decided that he had been responsible for my father's death by Pissing About instead of sending him Over Gravesend Hospital sooner where apparently they would have Sorted him in no time at all had he only got there early enough. All this was of course in the future and should not concern us at the moment because for the purposes of this particular narrative, Dr Outred still maintains his elevated position which was close to the Blessed Saints themselves.

In those days a number of family doctors did their own dispensing and ours was one of them. Patients were not handed their medicines at the time of consultation and were required to return for them later when they would be ready on the table in the general waiting room in rows of boxes and bottles labelled with names. This meant that typically by late afternoon the table hosted an interesting range of potions and multi-coloured pills awaiting collection by a steady stream of the sick or their envoys. It was a reasonably seamless system.

One particular visit to the surgery at De Warren House, London Road, stands out very well indeed because my mother for some reason wanted to speak to Dr Outred without me by her side and so she left me in the waiting room with a Beano comic to occupy me. As I was far too young to appreciate the pleasures of Beano it did not occupy me for very long. Many years later I came to understand that this consultation had something to do with my father recently being Home on Leave and some kind of nasty infection that had passed from him to her causing a certain amount of marital discord. It certainly caused my aunts shake their heads and speak of it in whispers once they became informed of it.

Strangely, on that chilly winter evening we were the only patients and when the Beano comic's attraction rapidly began to pall I turned my attention to the eye-catching array of medications awaiting collection. There were pills of every hue in some of the little glass bottles as well as the standard and exceedingly dull white ones and also tall bottles of red, blue and green tonics and cough mixtures. As I studied them it began to seem very unfair to me that some specifically selected people who were undoubtedly Special like the doctor himself, were given a whole bottle of red pills or blue ones whilst other lesser mortals were destined to merely receive the white ones. Some years later when Papa's Ice Cream Parlour Over-the-Town began to make a range of flavours once more, I likened this particular situation to being doled out vanilla ice cream when others were lucky enough to receive chocolate or strawberry because we all knew that vanilla was definitely not a real flavour at all but just another way of saying Plain. However that comparison was yet to come as at the time of my mother's tearful consultation Papa was still simply serving cups of tea and broken biscuits and I don't think I had experienced the joys of ice cream of any variety but that's probably beside the point.

That early winter evening in 1944 no matter which way I looked at it, I felt that a grave injustice was being done to some of Dr Outred's faithful followers so I decided with all the wisdom of a four-year-old, that it was up to me to bring some balance to the situation. With the waiting room still eerily empty I began a redistribution of the pills by first emptying all the containers and then methodically refilling them so that each recipient would now get at least one or two of the nicely coloured ones. Quite an effort was involved but by the time I had finished and turned my attention to the more complex problem of the bottled liquids, not one of the Northfleet sick that evening would suffer the indignity of having to swallow Vanilla Pills. Relishing my new role as a Junior Warrior for Justice I was in no doubt that they would be quite delighted although in the furthest recesses of my mind there began a slight uncertainty with regard to how the doctor himself might view the matter.

Almost as soon as that misgiving occurred to me I was left in no doubt as to his position on the matter and even after all these years I cannot easily forget the look of disbelief and fury on his face. I knew he was itching to take to me physically because his hands, at the level of my shoulders, clenched and unclenched as he hissed at me. He said that I was a totally irresponsible and ill-disciplined child and that my wayward behaviour would result in a lot of extra work for him. My mother, horrified and increasingly tearful, repeatedly apologised for me. That behaviour wasn't like me, apparently because usually I was as Good as Gold. He looked as if he doubted that and said something about me needing Much Firmer Guidance and she assured him she was going to Give Me What For when I got home. I rather imagined he seemed just a little placated when she said that.

She talked about the What For I was going to get all the way back along London Road and down Springhead Road which didn't make the walk home very pleasant, especially when she promised it would be the Hiding of my Life. I tried in vain to broach the issue of Natural Justice when it came to those who were unfairly doled out Vanilla Pills but she just didn't seem to be interested. Strangely, now I simply can't remember if I actually did get the Hiding that was said to lie in wait for me.

# A Navigation of Northfleet High Street

If we went shopping in Gravesend my mother always told us that we were going Over-the-Town and usually we took a bus there and back. Shopping in Northfleet meant we were going Down-The-High-Street and invariably we walked. When I was very young, perhaps five or six years old, this was quite a trek and my heart would sink at the thought but there was no point in arguing and suggesting a bus ride because I knew we weren't Made Of Money. Later, with my brother in the push chair it did not seem quite such a journey, especially if I was allowed to do the pushing on the long, flat bits. We would set off directly after our midday dinner armed with shopping bags, one made of string and that was the one I might be told to carry later.

In the time before my brother was born I was usually already complaining when we had barely walked up Springhead Road and reached The Hill where we might well Run Into a neighbour returning from the very same mission and this meant stopping for a chat. The chat one day with Grace Bennett was about bananas because Ripleys had them, causing great excitement and her Joan was going to have one on toast for her tea. The thing I remember most vividly about Ripleys is the woman with hair the colour of Kentish Cobnuts who smiled a great deal, flashing beguiling glimpses of gold teeth. I remember nothing of the bananas except being told that Joan Bennett getting a whole one on her toast meant she was Spoilt-Rotten but then everybody knew that was because she was now the Baby of the family.

On we walked, past Dr Crawford's surgery in Granby Place, past Horlocks garage and St Botolph's Vicarage, behind grey walls and almost but not quite hidden by trees and then to Council Avenue. Here we might very well stop again if we Ran Into Mrs Ditchburn who had a family connection with Ditchburn's Newsagency and not only that, a famous relative called Ted as well. Ted was goalkeeper for Tottenham Hotspur and much revered by all the boys I knew and most of their fathers. My mother greatly approved of Mrs Ditchburn and so the chat would be an extended one so Little Margery and I could play pretend hopscotch on the paving stones and I would admire her shiny black shoes and wish I had some just the same.

We then had to pass a number of very boring places like the Gas Board Showrooms and the Food Office that had something to do with Cod Liver Oil and free Orange Juice, both of which I treated with great suspicion, before we reached the High Street proper which I always felt started at the Wardona Cinema, and there my spirits lifted. In those days most cinemas showed two feature films plus a newsreel and sometimes a cartoon as well and the programme was changed at least twice a week. This meant the Wardona was a busy and exciting place but my mother disapproved of it because of possibly Catching Something from the seats as it wasn't very clean. The reason I liked the Wardona was because all my classmates and neighbours went to the Saturday Morning Children's Picture Show and once in a while, though not very often, I was allowed to join them. Oh the excitement of those Saturday mornings hemmed in on all sides by unruly screeching schoolchildren some with pre-schoolers in tow who, surprisingly and despite the noise level often fell asleep. For sixpence you got a full three hours of entertainment and came out with a thumping headache and possibly sometimes with nits. Sadly, years later after the expense of a complete upgrade and a Grand Opening featuring stars from a famous TV soap opera, the Wardona closed its doors for good. The Grand Opening had been a highlight in my early teenage life because although we did not at the time own a TV set ourselves, everyone else did and I had actually seen two episodes of The Grove Family Saga at the Bennetts in Buckingham Road, sitting with Joan who was still being Spoilt-Rotten whilst our mothers spoke in low voices of matters we must not be privy to. So the grand re-opening coming at a time when I felt I was destined to be a famous actress meant that I made sure I was first in line to smile and chat to the young girl who cut the ribbon and made the speeches and who I desperately yearned to emulate and whose name I now completely forget. I even featured in the extreme left corner of the photo that appeared in The Gravesend & Dartford Reporter which was of course totally thrilling.

However, long before the demise of the Wardona I always experienced a frisson of something like excitement when passing this particular area of the High Street because adjacent in the Astoria Dance Hall was Marjorie Slade's Dancing School where the especially fortunate girls in my class at school like Helen Gunner and Pearl Banfield went every Wednesday for Tap Dancing and sometimes on Saturday too for Ballet

Classes at one and sixpence a time. My mother would not be persuaded about the dance classes even though my cousin Pat from Crayford had been learning Tap for more than two years and now danced better than Ginger Rogers. No matter how good a dancer I was sure I would become I knew we had better things to do with our money.

By the time we were deep into the High Street proper I had usually stopped complaining about being tired and the shops themselves became all at once more interesting. We were sure to visit Treadwells the Butcher and Knowles the Baker followed by Pearsons the Grocer and then even Frosts simply to look at radios and electric bar heaters. Frosts was an exciting place because posters on the wall advised that Pianos were For Hire or Available on Hire Purchase. In addition they had Radio Sets & Components of every description and any Overhauls were carried out by Expert Workmen. What could be better than that? Sometimes we went inside to examine things and then Bernard might be allowed to get out of the pushchair provided that he was very good indeed which he usually was.

Occasionally we bought a few mint humbugs from Barratts where the old man and his daughter had sold sweets and cigarettes for years and where nearly a decade later he was to refuse to sell me a box of matches because I did not buy cigarettes to go with them and I threatened to report him to the conveniently nearby Police Station. He advised me to do my worst but when I did so the unhelpful sergeant at the desk told me that Old Barratt didn't have to sell anything to anyone if he didn't want to and that was the Law whether I liked it or not. I did not like it so some months after this unpleasant and to my mind most unfair interlude, disguised with sunglasses and a fake American accent, I ventured into Barratts again clutching tuppence in my right hand, glad to see the old man still there behind the counter. I asked him to weigh me up a quarter of a pound each of humbugs, toffees, sherbet lemons, liquorice allsorts and dolly mixtures which he did. I asked for half an ounce of Hearts of Oak and some Rizla cigarette papers together with twenty Players' Weights and – oh yes, as an afterthought and so, so casual – a box of matches please. This impressive range of potential purchases was now lined up neatly on the counter before me, Old Barratt looking as Old Nan would say, As-Pleased-As-Bleeding-Punch. I picked up the matches, placed the two pennies on the counter and said I'd changed my mind and I'd just have the matches today thank you before sauntering out into the sunshine of the High Street once more, heart pounding. He followed me only to the doorway which I found surprising, gesticulating and blaspheming . Of course I was much too cowardly to ever risk venturing onto the premises again. I thought it best not to mention any of this to anyone at the time.

    Back in 1949 a visit to Mrs. Bodycombe's hardware shop was a must on a Friday for Reckitts Blue for the coming Monday wash and then quite often we Dropped In on Little Nannie Constant in Hamerton Road to make sure she was all right and to drink a cup of tea, or in my mother's case, even two. In winter it would be nearly dark when we ventured up Station Road again and past the Old Mission Hall where if we were lucky we might hear the Northfleet Silver Band in rehearsal and I could stand for a few minutes transfixed to hear Rossini Overtures and John Philip Sousa Marches, music that mesmerised me. Fifty years later the same melodies at a band concert in Auckland, New Zealand were to conjure up immediate memories of Northfleet on a cold and frosty early evening, the long-gone buildings frozen somehow in both time and memory.

    The High Street in those days wasn't all shops by any means because a number of people actually lived there in brick houses facing the street, including Bill Moody who had a Coach business and ran it from his front room and had Been-There-For-Donkey's-Years. In the years following my father's death we sometimes took day tours with Moodys' to places like Brighton and Hastings, The Devil's Punch Bowl and Whipsnade Zoo. Surprisingly at twelve and thirteen I would more than likely be allowed to choose the trip and the one I remember most clearly was The Devil's Punch Bowl because of the endless Monica Edwards books I had read. Oh the excitement of driving by the very place where the mythical Thornton Family had their farm and rode their ponies and lived their fascinating lives! For a brief moment I imagined I could simply reach out and touch them. Bernard, younger and not having read the books was not nearly as enthralled and mostly slept the trips away because he couldn't see the purpose of them unless a bird of prey might be sighted.

    Homeward bound from High Street shopping meant walking on the river side of the street, dropping into Hardy's the Drapers and perhaps the huge and forbidding Post Office. Past the photographer where both my brother and I had our very first baby photographs taken, each of us five months old, proudly sitting all by ourselves in smocked white silk baby frocks and looking astonishingly alike. The same photographer where at the age of three I had yet another photo taken to be sent to my father in North Africa. Wearing my best blue satin dress inherited from my cousin Margaret I stare at the camera, unsmiling from beneath a fringe, newly trimmed for the occasion.

Datlen's always put out their Frying-Now notice in the early evening and the smell of freshly fried haddock and chips was so tantalising it brought tears to the eyes. But we always bought our Fish & Chips from Shepherd Street though possibly Datlen's wet fish might be scanned for suitability if it was a Friday. Very occasionally we might buy a pint of shrimps for tea from Edgeley's the shellfish shop nearby where they were measured in a pewter mug and firmly wrapped in newspaper then put into the very bottom of the string bag that I would now be assigned to carry, bumping uncomfortably against my legs. Less exciting was the Cooked Meats shop operated by Mr Davies who was the cousin of one of our neighbours and so had to be briefly chatted to if he was reasonably idle. I liked the grocery store with the musty sawdust smell where a Mrs. Lambert who had Been-There-Since-the-Year-Dot sold sterilised milk from Mortlock Dairy in tall glass bottles with interesting red and black stoppers which we never bought because my mother maintained it wasn't healthy and you never really knew what was in it. Aunt Mag told her she was wrong because it was Sterilised which meant it must be good and anyway she had used it herself for years with no ill effect. Mrs Lambert also sold salt in huge lumps that looked like ice which again we never bought because you didn't know whose hands had been all over it.

Bareham's the Barber was always busy and that's where my father usually went for his short back and sides and where he took my brother for his very first grown up haircut just before he started school in September 1951. Until then my mother trimmed his hair herself but on that early September day he strode off to Bareham's hand in hand with the father who was to die within months, like a Big Boy, the two of them on a trip together Bernard would years later remember no details of, no matter how hard he struggled to recall it. And struggle he did when he became middle aged and began to fully realise how that early loss had so significantly affected him especially as the day of the haircut was the day he was given the Penknife. It was quite an ordinary knife but extra special to our father since he had won it as a prize just before leaving school. Bernard at the age of four was speechless with delight to be given it even if he was quite incapable of opening the blades. For many years he kept it in the pocket of his shorts and from time to time at school it would be confiscated because knives were not supposed to be taken to school in the first place. Nevertheless, he always got it back, or nearly always because when he was fourteen it was confiscated by a police officer who said it was an Offensive Weapon. Then it was lost for all time in the plethora of items removed from teenage boys by police officers. He made several trips to Gravesend Police Station and attempts were made to find it but to no avail. He was still complaining of the loss in the year 2000.

But to return to Bareham's, once my mother booked in to the Ladies Department operated by Miss Joyce for a Toni Perm and I was allowed to wait while she had it and look at all the magazines and not make a nuisance of myself. I must have been at least nine or ten because I was certainly a good enough reader to be both shocked and not a little confused by the problem pages of the magazines of the day where writers asked the advice of Aunt Evelyn on such matters as How Much Intimacy To Allow My Fiancé Before Marriage and Why Do I Not Seem To Be Able To Conceive. I knew enough of the facts of life to understand that Conceiving had something to do with Falling-For-a-Baby and that was a topic that must not be discussed even though it could be seen as both a very good or a very bad thing depending upon the circumstances. I was definitely much more puzzled about what Intimacy might mean. As our household was not Made of Money we did not go in for magazines and so I rarely had the opportunity to familiarise myself with the contents. Later our Toni Perms were done by my Aunt Martha who had set up a little home business at half a crown a time and you bring your own perm kit only she didn't charge family. Aunt Martha did not provide magazines.

In those days Northfleet High Street was always a busy place with most of the businesses open until six o'clock – including Spooners the Florists, Rowes the Optician, Hinkley's Shoes and Fred Waters Gentlemen's Outfitters from London. Wherever possible, family members were employed by each enterprise with sons and daughters, nephews and nieces stepping behind counters after school and on Saturday mornings. Rayners

Hardware, for instance eventually provided employment for the whole family, the three sons Ken, Arnold and Eric and their sister Gwennie and the occasional cousin as well.

Walking home would often be cold, the temperature having dropped at least six or seven degrees since we set out but as it darkened, each building we passed took on a warm and welcoming look as lights were switched on and all the pubs began to open – The Edinburgh Castle, The Coopers' Arms, The Railway Tavern and The Marquis of Granby. Pete's Café on The Hill looked especially cheerful because as we approached it I knew we had conquered most of the journey. I longed to go inside but we never did, even when we had one of the Aunts or Old Nan with us because it was a place where only men gathered, always with vans and lorries parked outside and Pete himself inside in a Fair Isle pullover making the endless cups of tea and cutting the sandwiches.

Understandably I would be quite worn out by the time we reached York Road, feet aching more than they should because often I was walking in shoes that didn't quite fit. But whatever the adverse aspects of those long-ago weekly shopping trips they were full of incident, however trifling, that would be totally absent for those retracing our steps in this totally modern and far more impersonal age when it seems that most of the shops have completely disappeared along with those specific services that supported our working class way of life.

## Getting To Know the Neighbours

Nellie Constant always considered herself remarkably fortunate to have secured the rental for 28 York Road, Northfleet, terraced cottages built in an area curiously known in the nineteenth century as Barrack Field. She said the alternative had been a flat at The Overcliffe end of Pier Road, Gravesend and she had never really been keen on flats because half the time you didn't even get your own lav and she had never held with sharing. In York Road not only did she have her very own lavatory but also a little stone flagged yard where clothes could be mangled, hens could be kept and children, should she have any, and of course she did, could play safely. She was not an overly outgoing or sociable individual and so it took time to get to know the neighbours no matter how closely packed together we then lived but she soon became friendly with Old Mrs Bassent at No 27 and when I was very small avoided The Willis family on the other side of us at No 29. This latter antipathy involved several nappies that my mother claimed were stolen from her washing line by the Willis family matriarch who was the grandmother of my future best friend Molly. It seems probably more likely that they were borrowed for the latest Willis baby and simply failed to be returned

The Bassents had an adopted daughter called Ina who was living in Burch Road, Gravesend with her second husband and her vastly overweight daughter, Evelyn. At various times during my childhood Evelyn, who had a much nicer nature than I did, was my friend and grateful to be so, a fact that fed my ego when I was five and she was six. At some stage after the war, Mr Bassent died and his wife moved out to live with Ina and I never saw her or Evelyn again. They were soon replaced by The Newberrys, Charlie and Mary and two small daughters called Janice and Barbara. When the Newberry girls started school they had freshly washed and ironed dresses morning and afternoon because their mother's hobby seemed to be washing. Mary Newberry often washed and ironed into the small hours of the morning and because there were no machines to help shoulder the load, her hands were red, raw and blistered. My mother said she brought it upon herself, there was no doubt about that.

There were no children at No 26, just Mr & Mrs Morris and their adult son, Norman. Mrs Morris had TB and was described as being a Hopeless Case by my mother who always covered her mouth with her hand, and sometimes even with the corner of her apron, when standing at the gate in conversation with her. I was so frightened of catching TB that I always passed the Morris gate at top speed and without breathing. On one occasion when early on a Monday morning Mrs Morris gave the remains of her Sunday joint to the dog we owned at the time, I removed it from him fearful that he might catch the disease. He was not co-operative and I risked being bitten but I wrenched it off him all the same because in those days all children were aware of the dangers of TB.

The Finch family were at No 24 with their little boy David and later their adopted daughter Nova who my mother said might be the Ruin of Them because with adopted children you Never Knew. Mrs Finch did not altogether approve of me because on more than one occasion I encouraged David to play unacceptable games and expose what his mother called his Lily. They later moved out to a new Council house at Erith with three bedrooms and an inside bathroom, close to the trolley bus stop. The Laytons replaced them, Cis with her grown up son Ramon, her second husband Bill and their young daughter Little Jeannie. Cis was a large and affable person and quickly made my mother her closest friend, swapping paperback love stories and confidences about men that were whispered during their frequent afternoon tea drinking sessions and which, irritatingly, I could neither hear nor comprehend.

Those living further up the street always remained a mystery to me although No 19 was I think the residence of May and John Bardoe and May's sister, Amy. May and Amy were so alike they must have been twins and also in the house were two well-behaved girls, Vera and Audrey. At some stage John Bardoe had a work place accident gossiped about locally for months and said by some to be murder although finally whoever was responsible was charged merely with manslaughter. The only other family I recall with clarity were the Banfields at No 7, Doug and Hilda and their two children Pearl and Derek. Hilda strived valiantly to ensure that the children kept themselves a little apart from the rest of us. This was not an easy task but I never knew them to be allowed out playing on the street or taking part in collecting for the Guy and usually they had their own Guy Fawkes celebration in their own garden. Neither did the family ever indulge in any kind of field work, even Hop Picking. My mother called them Toffee Nosed.

The Giles family lived further down the street towards Springhead Road at No 30 with several grown up daughters, Ada, Amelia, Edith & Grace. The girls, who all looked alike to me, knitted socks for soldiers during the war years and put notes inside them hoping to catch a husband which made my mother sniff disapprovingly a great deal and say they were desperate. For one of them at least, this strategy worked beautifully and in 1946 she married a rather overweight soldier whose name I've forgotten and rented a house opposite us where on account of her culinary ministrations he gained even more weight.

The house I knew best and was to visit most frequently as I grew was No 31 where Molly Freeman lived with her big sister Pam and younger brother Georgie. Ivy Freeman was a small woman with admirable posture who always wore high heels. It was rumoured she had been a maid in a Big House and she certainly spoke well and knew how a table should be laid though the family were clearly on the same level of poverty as ourselves. My mother for some reason best known to herself claimed to be scandalised to find Ivy Freeman ordered coke from the Hardy's delivery man rather than coal though why she thought this was any business of hers is hard to know. She also criticised the family for having newspaper on the kitchen table seven days a week. It should be pointed out that at 28 we had a proper cloth on Sundays which undoubtedly placed us in a slightly elevated position on the social scale. Apart from this, apparently the Freeman children did not have proper blankets on their beds in winter and were allowed to Race the Streets on Sundays whereas I was only permitted to read a library book or play Ludo once I had come back from Mass. Naturally enough I envied them their Sunday freedom and would not have minded about the lack of blankets.

Next door to Molly lived Aunt Maudie Obee who was a very elderly lady dressed always in black and not really anyone's aunt. She lived alone in her little house surrounded by china knick-knacks from days out long ago to Margate and Southend and grew vegetables and made Parsnip Wine. On one occasion she gave us a bottle to celebrate some major occasion but my mother poured it into an outside drain once darkness fell and told her later it had been delicious. Ernie & Flo Eves lived at No 35 with a grown up son and when our father died she gave Mickey Mouse and Donald Duck soap in gift boxes to my brother and myself and when he lunged towards Mickey, reprimanded Bernard and said he must let his sister choose first like a gentleman. I was greatly impressed.

The Hinkleys who repaired cars and later ran a taxi service lived at 37 on the corner and by the time my brother was born always had gleaming black vehicles parked in the small space beside the house. Opposite them was the corner shop run by Hilda Sims and although we saw it as our very own York Road shop I think more properly the address was in Springhead Road. Sims's Shop sold most things that were available during the war years but later specialised in newspapers, magazines, ice cream and jars of sweets. Molly and Georgie had a weekly order with them for comics such as Film Fun and Rainbow and their mother took Picture Post and Reveille all of which were later usually passed on to us, my mother protesting each time that it wasn't necessary. Whilst turning the pages of Picture Post on Sunday afternoons she was often heard to mutter comment that a lot of money was wasted in the Freeman family. Meanwhile, I was more than thankful for this particular habit of extravagance and vowed that when I grew up I was definitely going to squander money.

## Among Our Souvenirs

Strange to reflect upon the knick-knacks we collect over the years, little bits and pieces that remind us of happy times, significant moments we are reluctant to relinquish. I seemed to grow up surrounded by such souvenirs, small mementos of noteworthy instances in life that presumably served to lend my mother a glimpse back to times past. The most precious of these lived on the mantelpiece above the kitchen stove that she considered to be a Victorian eyesore and couldn't wait to replace with what was called a Tiled Surround and was Modern. But I loved the stove, black and solid in its chimney alcove and I never entirely adjusted to its insipidly pink and pale replacement when it finally arrived.

The kitchen mantle was the place for the reassuring paraphernalia of daily life, the trappings of a working class presence firmly placed in the middle of the twentieth century. Items evoking less poignant memories of days gone by were positioned on the Front Room mantelpiece, that room accessed immediately from the street and hurried through by all in their haste to reach the warmth and security of the kitchen. It was only in later years I paused to consider it odd that her wedding photographs were consigned there.

The little china ornament importantly announcing that it was A Present From Margate sat always in the kitchen warmth, its base of reproduction sea shells losing colour over the decades but regularly prompting the story of the summer day of its purchase. It was a day she would always find difficult to forget because it had definitely been her sister Mag's idea to lend her the old blue shoes in the first place on account of the smart new ones she had just bought in the market and Mag was determined to wear those new ones come hell or high water to impress her new husband. Well they must have been newly-weds, Mag and Harold, as there were definitely no babies as yet to be cared for while they all, the four of them, skedaddled to the coast for the day on the early train and their little Harold had come ever so quickly after the wedding. Very premature little soul he'd been. The Four of them had been Mag and her Harold together with his brother Les and of course Nellie. Even before the lunchtime pint and cheese sandwich at that pub along the Front in Marine Gardens, she thought it was called The Elephant, Mag was Creating Something Awful and saying that her feet Was Killing Her. Demanded her old blue shoes back and wanted Nellie to wear the new ones if you don't mind! Would you credit it? But that was Mag all over. There'd been a right set-to outside the pub with Mag saying well who did the old blue shoes belong to in the first place? And her Harold joined in too, well he would wouldn't he? The long and the short of it had been that Nellie was forced to give the shoes up and walk around for the rest of the day in Mag's new ones that really crippled her. So it hadn't been much of an outing except she'd won a box of chocolates at Dreamland and on their way back to the station she'd bought the little china ornament – A Present from Margate. Les had wanted to buy it for her but she didn't think he was much cop, not a patch on her

Poor Fred, so she bought it herself which really gave him The Pip.

The grey and white porcelain kitten playing with the ball of wool was another seaside purchase and had come from Southend in the summer of 1939 just before she had, with a certain degree of reluctance, married our father at the Catholic Church in Crayford, thus ensuring that Bernard and I should be born. Off they had gone on his motor bike to sample the delights of a day by the sea. It was he who had bought it on this occasion along with a manicure set. He had laughed, shuffled his feet a bit in the motor cycle boots and talked about Plighting His Troth. She hadn't entirely understood the term but had a good grasp of what he meant by it. Well she wasn't completely daft after all was she? Later Mag and Old Nan had nearly piddled themselves laughing at the manicure set because she hadn't got no nails of course; bitten to the bone they were and had been ever since Poor Fred Went. By rights it was Poor Fred she should have married of course and they'd been properly engaged for several years before the TB took him but then he would not have wanted to see her On the Shelf would he? She had loved him dearly. Once or twice she showed me the special card he had given her on the occasion of her twenty-fifth birthday, ivory satin with red and gold lettering. It was wrapped in tissue paper. Inside he had written To My Sweetheart From Fred. Her hands trembled ever so slightly when she handled it.

So it hadn't been easy to marry Bernard Joseph Hendy and in the days before the wedding she had discussed the momentous decision more than once with Mag, and sometimes also with Maud and Martha because after all that's what sisters were for and blood's thicker than water. In terms reminiscent of the young Diana Spencer in a time that was yet to come she reminded herself and her siblings that he was a Good Man and didn't drink nor use bad language. Her sisters anxiously observed their bridesmaids' dresses and enthusiastically agreed and so of course did her mother, reminding her that The Bleeding Church was Booked and calling her a Silly Mare Who Didn't Know Her Arse From Her Elbow. And so in August of 1939 the wedding duly took place and although the photographs of the event were to live always in the chill of the Front Room, the porcelain kitten played happily with his ball of wool on the kitchen mantelpiece from that day forward. She couldn't for the life of her remember what had happened to the manicure set though.

  The cobalt blue vases and little jug decorated with enamelled flowers had been given to our parents by Great Aunt Martha who lived near the station in Northfleet and always appeared to me to be very, very old indeed. My mother admitted once or twice that at the time she was given them she couldn't honestly admit to being as Keen as Mustard but Great Aunt Martha had said they were antique and known as Bristol Glass and hard to come by. Nellie was not altogether taken with antiques but my father had investigated the history of Bristol Glass which by the time they received them was an art that had almost died out and it was his belief that they should be treasured as one day they might well be Worth Something. And as Great Aunt Martha was a frequent visitor they were kept always in pride of place in the kitchen and over the years my brother and I became fond of them and most reluctant for them to be sold when this was suggested by Old Nan after the death of our father at a time when we were particularly short of the readies.

The kitchen at York Road was where we routinely made our rag rugs each winter to replace those so worn they had to be discarded. Old clothing was harvested and laboriously cut into strips then pegged onto squares of sacking. Such an easy task that a child of five could learn to master it, and did so. We sat in the dying firelight on winter evenings from November to February and worked whilst listening to the radio – Life with the Lyons, Journey Into Space, Round the Horne and Meet the Huggetts. And of course the fruits of our joint labours were seen as a necessary winter pastime rather than possible future mementos of days gone by. I had completely forgotten about Rag Rugs and our annual ritual of producing them until I visited Bernard's house in Lincolnshire decades later. I came face to face with one once again in his Lincolnshire study, neatly settled on polished wood and announcing its presence with riotous colours. Then I was at once aware how overwhelmingly powerful are these mementos that connect us to the past. Instantaneously I was propelled back into that long ago kitchen at 28 York Road, and harked back with longing to a time that had gone forever and would never return.

Later I realised that my brother had kept safe all those knick-knacks and keepsakes of our mother's and I was suffused with gladness, a hard to describe delight akin to love for A Present From Margate and a Porcelain Kitten. And the most agonizing tug on the heart was unquestionably for the ivory satin card with red and gold lettering – To My Sweetheart From Fred. The tissue paper had gone though but when I closed my eyes I could still recall how it fluttered to the tremble of my mother's fingers.

# The Sad Passing of Playing With Fire

I can barely remember my first Guy Fawkes Night but I have been told that it was in 1946 when a few rudimentary squibs and sparklers had once more become available following the scarcity the war had occasioned. I was still an Only Child when I stood with my father at the periphery of the blazing bonfire on the Old Green, tightly holding his hand, wanting very much to love him as much as I loved my mother, and marvelling at the way the flames licked up into the darkness. Later he lit sparklers and balanced them on the back gate because I was much too fearful to hold them and wanted my mother to light them rather than him. But of course now we were a Proper and Complete Family again the overseeing of playing with fire was henceforth the responsibility of men.

Re-establishing the place of fathers returning from the years of conflict was difficult for some children who had been babies when the men left and ready for school when they returned. I was unquestionably one of them and longed for my father to simply return to Africa, the land he seemed to have come to love so much and told so many stories about. Overall though, the War had been but an interruption to the established order of the rituals and traditions of the children of North Kent and by November 1946 the juvenile calendar was slowly and determinedly being restored to its natural rhythm. My Grandmother had the previous year unilaterally decided to resurrect A Pinch & A Punch For The First Of The

Month and astonished me with what I saw as an unprovoked act of aggression on the first of June that year, the day before my birthday. I was somewhat mollified to find that I had license to respond with A Pinch & A Kick For Being So Quick! I imagine that today's five-year-olds might be totally bewildered by this rather odd monthly practice and am still confused as to why it spent those war years asleep.

Over the decades similarly harmless customs seem to have been abandoned in favour of television, tablets and mobile telephones and this was certainly so by 1950 when most of England no longer indulged in Well Dressing and Whit Walks. Not everyone was content at the departure of familiar community customs. My mother and aunts spoke fondly of a time when Empire Day really mattered and all children were given flags and sang Land of Hope and Glory. Old Nan maintained that the streets of East London were decorated with bunting and stories were told about those who had displayed courage like Clive of India. By the time I was attending school the day was but a shadow of its former self with not a flag in sight.

On the other hand, as I grew older, Valentine's Day still created a flurry of interest even in the very young. We were all anxious to receive a card from an anonymous admirer and at times were even forced to invent one and deliver a card surreptitiously to ourselves. This was not a problem for me as I invented a great many scenarios in which I had a starring role but those who lived in families with a stricter regard for Truth might have struggled.

Back then mothers seemed generally adept at producing pancakes and no child I knew of would willingly have relinquished Shrove Tuesday, a festival that appeared to be unquestionably deep-rooted, yet has largely vanished without trace. Coming home after school to pancakes doused with sugar and lemon juice was a treat to be looked forward to for days in advance.

Ash Wednesday on the other hand, could be more readily discarded especially by those from non-religious households. April Fool's Day was another matter altogether. The tricks, some more elaborate and amusing than others, could be planned weeks in advance particularly by boys. Chocolate Eggs to celebrate Eastertide were easily re-established after the war and became mandatory as they remain. There were times, disappointingly, when they were replaced with more mundane coloured eggs when chocolate proved too expensive. The rather more tedious Maypole dancing to celebrate May Day was disappearing by the time I was a teenager and I don't remember too many tears at its demise although I now feel a twinge of sadness at its loss in the same way as I half-heartedly mourn the passing of Morris Dancers. We also, rather strangely, seemed to take an enormous interest in The Boat Race though none of us knew anyone who had gone anywhere near the University towns of Oxford and Cambridge. We chose our team with enthusiasm and listened avidly to the race on the radio.

As far as Halloween is concerned, these days growing in popularity, we seemed to live in a county where this was celebrated by roughly half of the child population and ignored by the rest. In North Kent we knew it as All Saints Night but it was mostly disregarded because we were already concentrating on the imminent and much more exciting Guy Fawkes celebrations. These were centred on almost every spare piece of waste ground so the bomb sites that proliferated in and around Northfleet were ideal venues. There was always a bonfire on The Old Green, and another one in Buckingham Road. The Old Green fire was controlled by the Ribbins and Bardoe boys ably assisted by most of the local girls. Our Guy making was for several years dominated by Colin Bardoe, who had a twin called Alan and an older brother called Kenny, all were boys with a certain amount of organizational skill. Colin was a resourceful and imaginative boy who aspired to hairdressing or choreography and longed to own a pony. He demonstrated a preference for the company of girls at a very young age and by the time we were nine several of us were already in love with him.

 He structured the procedures involved for the celebration of Guy Fawkes with military precision. Old clothes were purloined from wherever we could find them and we sat as an admiring audience as he turned them into an Edwardian Gentleman with a little help from Molly Freeman and Pat Turner. For the ten days or so before the Fifth of November we toured the streets with the Guy in an old pram, accosting passers-by and knocking on doors in order to collect as much money as possible. At the same time as begging for A Penny For The Guy and hoping for sixpence we chanted lustily Guy, Guy, Stick Him In The Eye, Chuck Him On The Bonfire & There Let Him Die. I suppose these days you might describe this particularly persistent endeavour as

Begging in the Streets and it would undoubtedly cause concern on Radio Talk Programmes and even local Councillors might be driven to comment. Back then it was simply harmless fun.

The money collected, and it was at times a reasonable sum certainly enough to make my mother purse her lips and Tut Tut, would then be spent on fireworks for the great day. Squibs, Bangers and Rockets, Roman Candles and Catherine Wheels, the bigger the better. The fireworks themselves were usually chosen by a small group headed by Alan and Colin and kept in their shed once they promised, Crossing their Hearts and Hoping to Die, that they would not let a single one off in advance of the Fifth. But they did, of course, in order to Test Them. Those early winter evenings leading up to the fifth were regularly punctuated with explosions and unlike today the neighbours never complained though my mother, egged on by my Grandmother, always pointed out that Them Bardoe Boys Couldn't Be Trusted. We did not totally agree with her but just in case our joint efforts came to nothing, we each had a few bangers and certainly some sparklers of our own on hand.

By the afternoon of the fifth the excitement reached fever pitch as we all waited breathlessly for it to get dark enough for the ritual to start. And always we began far too early of course, with sparklers to entertain the very youngest, those who could barely walk and babies in push chairs. By eight o'clock the streets would be aflame with Catherine Wheels and Roman Candles and the sky fiery with rockets. For days the bonfire itself would have been growing ever more vast as families ransacked their cupboards and outhouses for anything combustible to add to it. At long last the Guy himself was hoisted to the top of the pyramid with the help of some of the fathers, the fire doused with paraffin and by nine the resulting blaze would send us into a frenzy. Colin would be leading the chant of Remember, Remember the Fifth of November, Gunpowder, Treason and Plot… whilst Alan and Kenny fought over the last of the rockets.

On one memorable occasion an observing teenage son of a particularly hard wing Protestant family shocked my father by trying to teach us a jingle that began: 'A Penny Loaf to Feed the Pope, A Faggot of Sticks to Burn Him…' and was chased back into the depths of Springhead Road before he could further corrupt the Good Catholics amongst us.

In these more modern times of tame and bland Council Firework Displays it's hard to convey the excitement of a Guy Fawkes celebration that has been essentially devised and choreographed by children themselves. Even when the last rocket had been launched and the initial ferocity of the fire had died down the excitement was not over. It was then that quantities of potatoes were thrown into the embers and Little Kathleen's mother from the row of Cottages opposite The Old Green, usually grimly unapproachable and somehow worn down by the care of her one child plus what were rumoured to be Unnatural Marital Demands, always made enough toffee apples for everyone!

During those years there were strangely few warnings from our parents about the dangers of playing with explosives and local shops were more than happy to sell what are now seen as highly hazardous products to their youngest customers. The annual gala event on November Fifth each year was passively accepted even though the occasional child did meet with more than a trivial accident. Burns were considered routine as long as they did not require specialised medical treatment. On one occasion Sandra Ribbins was taken to Dr Crawford on the sixth with a nasty burn to her hand and, even more alarming, Joan Bennet claimed that her cousin Muriel had a neighbour who almost lost the sight of one eye when a Catherine Wheel chose to spin off the garden gate. This may or may not have been completely accurate as Joan was prone to exaggeration and in any case such incidents though sobering were viewed pragmatically and seen as almost certain to happen from time to time when children and explosives coincide.

It could simply be that back in the 1940s and 1950s we were of necessity a more street-wise and aware group although I always saw myself as fearful and not one willing to take unnecessary risks. Certainly putting ourselves into the kind of situations that are heavily legislated against today, resulted in very few mishaps and we would have greeted the idea of a fireworks ban with uncomprehending astonishment. Luckily for us Health & Safety Requirements as we now know them were still just a seed of awareness in the ghostly intellect of grey shadow people yet to be born.

## Black Hands & Smoky Tea

I'd quite forgotten the power of that oh so distinctive fragrance of hops until a casual acquaintance brought it back to mind recently with an incidental internet comment. How could I have neglected for so long the characteristic aroma so unique that just one whiff will fling the recipient directly into bygone Septembers in the Kentish countryside? How efficiently the sense of smell works on our most basic emotions to trigger memories from long ago. And the odd scent of hops is particularly vibrant, bringing me always back to a pause in effort and exertion in those late summer afternoons when my Grandmother and Aunts clasped mugs of smoky tea produced by my mother with hands black from harvesting.

George Orwell on one of his Life Among The Poor projects in the 1930s maintained that Hop Picking was far from being a holiday and as far as remuneration was concerned in his opinion no worse employment existed. He complained bitterly about his stained hands, his cracked fingers and made no comment at all concerning that idiosyncratic aroma that is capable of bringing tears to the eyes of the rest of us. For we ex-hoppers, Going Hopping will remain always an experience so idyllic we struggle to find words adequate for the description of it.

Our mother's family The Constants in all their diversity could definitely be described as enthusiastic agricultural workers. This was primarily due to the influence of our grandmother who was never happier than when she was harvesting the earth's bounty. Digging for potatoes had an agreeable effect upon her general demeanour and the sight of orderly rows of peas and beans seemed to somehow bring out the best in her. This affection for the freedoms involved in part-time Field Work had definitely been passed down to our mother and her siblings so that they would as one descend upon the pea fields of North Kent with a certain fervour as soon as the season began. They signed up for Piecework with a strange mixture of gratitude and belligerence that was the hallmark of those who clearly saw themselves as independent contractors of the Lower Orders.

The Constant Family produced exceptionally reliable seasonal workers who applied themselves diligently throughout weather that was at times hardly indicative of summer and at the same time they largely enjoyed the solid, earthy labour they turned their attention to. Old Nan maintained that you couldn't beat a good stable week or two with the Pea Bines even though all the bending played Merry Hell with her back. Ten days of Soft Fruits also earned her seal of approval and she was even capable of waxing lyrical over a yield of onions. However, all fruits and vegetables paled into insignificance when put alongside the annual event of Going Hopping and it mattered little that the hops themselves were not traditionally consumed until they had been turned into beer. Old Nan could become passionate indeed about hops and never took her eye off the ball for a moment as far as their harvesting was concerned. In mid-August the excitement mounted because they were now very nearly ready for picking and all members of the family not otherwise engaged on more urgent business would be ready and willing to pick them. There were usually about twenty of us. My grandmother together with Motherless Little Violet, Aunt Martha with Pat, Aunt Maud with June and Desmond, Aunt Mag and Uncle Harold with young Harold, Leslie, Margaret and Ann, Freda with baby Susan, Uncle Edgar and wife with daughter Daphne, and of course my mother, brother and me – all of us could be found emerging from the pickers' train at Maidstone station poised for six weeks of hard toil and high adventure.

I no longer remember the name of Our Farm but the memories surrounding the weeks of rural freedom are still astonishingly vivid. In the 1940s a family of two adults and two children could earn between three and four pounds a week which meant a grand total of perhaps twenty or thirty pounds by the end of the season which was enough to make a great deal of difference to the budgets of families such as ours. One of the conditions of employment was that the hoppers must remain for the full term of the harvest and to ensure this half the earnings were retained and paid as a lump sum at the end of September. Sometimes only tokens were distributed during the period of picking and these could be spent in the local village, both to purchase supplies from the shop and also, more importantly, supplies at the pub. The nearest pub was visited regularly by the adults on Friday and Saturday nights and by my uncles and my grandmother most nights. Sometimes we children would be sent off to purchase bottles of beer from the off-licence and these were consumed in the cookhouse after dinner by those who remained behind. Beer or no beer, sitting in the cookhouse watching the firelight dance and flicker after the meal was eaten is not easily forgotten. Nobody minded how long the children stayed up, and even when we did drift off to bed, we could hear the comforting refrains of *Nellie Dean, My Old Dutch* and *Waiting At The Church*, long into the night. But it was up promptly at five the next morning when the day's work began and being a child did not automatically exclude you from the hard work; we were all expected to stand at the bins and pick despite the soporific effect of the plants. However, our mother and aunts were generally agreeable to letting us finish our contribution at noon each day when the only child still required to continue working, was Motherless Little Violet who, most unfortunately for her, was being brought up by Old Nan. She was an exacting caregiver and consequently Little Violet despite her tender years sometimes picked all day and fell asleep exhausted at six pm each evening. But the afternoons were playtime for the rest of us and we roamed the local villages and woodland in a shabby, disparate group, gathering cobnuts and berries and daily becoming less and less popular with the villagers. The older boys were adept at purloining hop tokens from the adults and these we could exchange for treats at the village store. Even once the war was officially over the return of treats such as ice cream and sweets was slow but strange items were on sale specifically to attract the young – Liquorice Wood for example, and Locust Beans and other delicacies that would no doubt cause most of us to shudder these days. I distinctly recall that the

Locust Beans were full of little maggots but I knocked them back with abandon despite that.

Each year without fail, the story of our mother's unconventional entry into the world as a somewhat premature infant, was retold by my grandmother, and we all became familiar with the details. That she had Come Early and was such a tiny little thing, no bigger than a milk jug, that she had been Born in a Caul that had been sold to a sailor in Whitstable a day or two later, for luck because as everybody knew, the owner of a Caul would never die by drowning. And that the trauma of the sudden birth Put Paid to Picking for the rest of the day though the new mother was Fit as a Fiddle again the next.

And at this stage our Grandmother, not generally known for her sentiment, could actually be seen to have a tear or two in her eye. There could be no doubting that she was never happier than in the hop gardens with her family all around her, telling tales of yesteryear as she deftly nipped the buds from garlands of bine into the bin. We, a larger group by far than those around us, always managed to pick more than other families and moved rapidly enough along the drifts, or alleyways of plants, day after day to make the tally men wary and other pickers resentful. But hostility never worried Nan because she said Bugger the Lot of Them and it was just Bleeding Jealousy that was their problem.

It was in the hop gardens at Mereworth that I first began to recognise that there was something distinctly different about our family. As I grew older and more street wise this knowledge established itself firmly into what was clearly evident. We were not just Working

Class Poor; we were certainly not part of the Respectable Working Class Poor. We were not respectable or reputable in any way. Not a single one of us was highly regarded or well thought of. We were the very opposite of Decent, Good and Upright. As a bunch we were undoubtedly untrustworthy, unreliable and devious. When we cheerfully appeared, Mob-Handed into any situation it was not long before mutterings of Riff Raff and even Diddicais tripped from the tongues of the more traditionally poor.

It was clear that these whispers at times caused our mother more concern than she was prepared to admit as she struggled to meet our father's expectations for us and give us just a little more than she had herself as a child. She would have been undoubtedly uncomprehending of the satisfaction Bernard was to later take in what he called Our Pikey Roots. But of course that pride was only to emerge when decades had passed and he owned Cape Wrath Lodge and a Bentley and had friends among the rich and influential.

Despite our undoubted position at the very Bottom of the Heap, over those post-war years we picked hops with both fervour and fortitude. The six-week season also served as a time of familial bonding when we cousins, at each other's throats for the rest of the year, mostly rubbed along together with an unusual degree of tolerance. The only young Constants conspicuous by their absence from these annual events were Tommy, Sandra and Paul, who belonged to Aunt Rose and were never allowed to join us. This was because Aunt Rose had the misfortune to be married to Uncle Mervyn who was Welsh and a serving officer in the Air Force which caused him to be Up His Own Arse. Even Aunt Mag agreed that he was a Snotty Nosed Git and my grandmother maintained he was raising his children to be Little Tight Arses. They were to be pitied having a father who denied them a free six-week break in the country every year but then Mervyn, on top of believing himself to be better than the next man, was tight fisted – so mean he wouldn't Give His Shit to the Crows.

    We went into collective mourning in the early 1950s when the ritual Country Holiday became a thing of the past as the majority of farms quite suddenly became totally mechanised. I was about thirteen or fourteen years old and Bernard was perhaps seven when we completed our final picking season. But for several years afterwards our Grandmother and aunts would regularly take trips into the local countryside, vainly visiting farms to make forlorn but hopeful enquiries as to whether pickers were needed. Sadly, they never were.

# Food, Glorious Food of the Forties & Fifties

Bernard agreed with me when I said it was odd to think that ordinary run-of-the-mill Roast Chicken was once so revered that for us, and for most of our neighbours, it was Christmas Dinner, and everybody knows Christmas Dinner is the most special meal of the year. He only half remembered us keeping fowl in the backyard in the late 1940s but we did, along with most of our neighbours; a belligerent rooster and a harem of hens, Rhode Island Reds. Other people kept Leghorns which were not nearly as reliable as Layers, at least that's what my father told me early in 1947. Even more importantly, I learned that our birds originated in America because that was where Rhode Island was and I imagined them making the sea trip under the care of Shaw Savill.

The Bassents next door kept rabbits and fattened them for eating which I didn't like to think about too much, preferring the slimline version my older cousins shot down by Crayford Creek and occasionally shared with us. Occasionally, particularly on allotments, some people kept pigs. It was frowned upon to keep them in backyards because of the smell and there might even have been a law against it.

As the years progressed the much-esteemed Roast Fowl lost its place at the top of the pyramid of prized foods and simply became a choice for Sunday dinner. At the same time families like the Scutts of Springhead Road, who our mother regarded as decidedly Uppity, had already announced they were having Turkey for Christmas! So the formerly greatly-favoured bird slid inexorably downwards, its demise coinciding with the opening of the Chicken Inn chain in the mid 1950s. One by one all the Aunts led by Old Nan in her best hat and coat boarded the Saturday 11.10 Express to Charing Cross specifically for the thrill of a Chicken Dinner in Leicester Square at 2/3d apiece. It was several months before our mother could be persuaded to join them because generally speaking she didn't hold with London, mostly because of the prices, but by the mid 1950s she had to admit that what with chicken still being quite dear in Gravesend, and when you added in the cost and the palaver of the cooking of it, an occasional 2/3d was not too steep. In any case whichever way you looked at it you had to admit it was a Day Out and everyone needed a Day Out from time to time and apart from all that, depending on what you ordered you could find an entire Chicken Leg on your plate together with roast potatoes, peas and gravy so you couldn't complain. These days the bird has simply settled into becoming a midweek dinner choice whether roasted, poached or more imaginatively turned into a curry and the heyday of the Chicken Inn chain is long gone.

    Children of the late 1940s were accustomed to a diet that has largely disappeared and we were totally ignorant of foods that today's child is completely familiar with. None of us had the slightest clue as to what a Kebab might be and although we might have heard of Pizza and perhaps even associated it with Italy that was as far as it went. Wimpy Bars were still firmly in the future along with Golden Egg restaurants and Chinese Takeaways.

We would have been quite confused by a Big Mac, possibly associating it with some kind of rainwear. The only takeaway meal we were completely at ease with was Fish & Chips, an option that had been around since the middle of the nineteenth century. Nellie who was born in 1908 remembered Fish & Chips as an occasional treat before WW1 and her own mother spoke of the Fish & Chips in Bethnal Green with almost a tear in her eye. According to the Aunts, we who were growing up in the 1940s were a great deal better off food-wise than they who had been born back in late-Edwardian England. As a group they did not always agree with regard to matters concerning the past but as far as food was concerned they were in total accord. Their parents being afflicted with drunkenness, they were of necessity forced to become accustomed to hunger pains.

Fashions in food together with the availability of some items dictate that the culinary experiences of each generation will differ. For instance delicacies chosen to impress and prepared in advance of a Saturday visit by relatives in the 1940s and 1950s would undoubtedly be a mystery to those born after 1960. Nevertheless the memory of the forward planning for such delights as Brawn or Jellied Eels is still vivid to me and was also readily recalled by my brother. Old Nan always referred to Brawn as Head Cheese but confusingly it bore little resemblance to any kind of cheese we were familiar with. Usually I was sent to the butcher to order the pig's head a few days in advance and told not to forget to ask him to split it and on these important errands invariably accompanied by my young and excited brother. For Saturday eating we would be sent back to collect it before school on Thursday. Then it would be squashed into the biggest cauldron we possessed along with salt, onion and carrots and simmered on the scullery stove all day until the water was disgustingly gelatinous and as my cousin Pat observed, just like snot when you've got a really bad cold. By teatime the gas would have been turned off, all corners of the house would smell of boiled pig and the cauldron contents left to cool enough for the remains of the head to be pulled forth after tea and the meat patiently picked from the bones. I usually tried to dodge any assistance with this even if it meant electing to go to bed earlier than usual but Bernard was always willing to help. By Friday evening both the meat and the liquid it had simmered in would be distributed among a number of receptacles and would long have set into typically unstable Brawn-like consistency, all ready to be consumed next day by the visiting relatives along with a dousing of vinegar and bread and margarine, always referred to as bread and butter. Nothing horrified me more than having to sample it but the adults did so with gusto and Bernard did with just a modicum of caution. I would simply be sent to the off licence together with my cousins Pat and June for bottles of Light Ale to accompany it.

I was less unsettled by Jellied Eels with the possible exception of the first part of the preparation and Bernard maintained that he positively enjoyed them but also baulked at the preparation. Everybody knew that to do the job properly you had to buy the eels not just fresh but definitely alive. We usually bought ours in Northfleet High Street after school and carried them home threshing around at the bottom of a shopping basket. I dreaded their approaching slaughter, not because I felt particularly concerned for their lives but because after chopping, the bits carried on wriggling, fascinating my horrified brother. Once an almost whole eel escaped before total execution and had to be salvaged from beneath the copper while its tail still fidgeted on the table.

The squirming pieces were dropped into boiling water with salt, diced onion and bay-leaves and simmered until after tea when they were left to cool ultimately to be served in much the same manner as the Brawn. By Saturday I would have put the demise of the unfortunate creatures aside enough to sample a small helping. Our Grandmother was particularly fond of them and without fail every time she ate them told the story of how she was once friendly with Tubby Isaacs of Aldgate when he first opened his famous stall just after the First War and how he had passed it on to his nephew Solly in 1939 before the Second War and ran off to America in case the Germans won. This was on account of them being Jewish apparently but we had no Jewish neighbours and little understanding of what being Jewish entailed. Nobody could make Jellied Eels like Tubby Isaacs she maintained. And maybe she was right because I wasn't overly fond of my mother's version but then as a child I was somewhat choosy about all food, seafood in particular, favouring shrimps over everything else available at the time.

On Sunday afternoons the Shrimp Man trundled through the local streets with his pushcart, sometimes offering crabs along with the shrimps, cockles, and whelks all sold by the half pint or pint measured in variously sized pewter jugs. If our mother felt the budget didn't run to shrimps I was happy to settle for cockles but never whelks whilst Bernard was game for anything. We only ever bought half a pint of shrimps for me and my brother but as my parents always favoured whelks anyway, they usually bought a pint or two to share between them. Occasionally as a special treat we might have a crab but not very often.

Another food hawker was the Pease Pudding & Faggots man who usually came on a Friday or Saturday but wasn't as reliable as the Shrimp Man. I was particularly fond of Pease Pudding which appeared to be quite harmlessly made from split yellow peas but not quite as keen on the Faggots especially after I once witnessed Aunt Martha making them out of very fatty bits of pork belly and an evil smelling pig liver. She said she didn't hold with buying them off the street because you didn't know what was in them. There didn't seem to be an appropriate response to that comment but I never forgot it.

The gastronomic highlight of our week was Sunday dinner which would always consist of a piece of roast Lamb or Beef together with roast potatoes, boiled potatoes, cabbage, carrots and gravy made with Bisto granules. Afters would most likely be Stewed Plums and Custard in summer and Prunes or an occasional Treacle Pudding in winter. There would be at least two other meaty meals during the week, cheap cuts such as Neck of Lamb which would be made into a stew with dumplings or possibly Pork Belly or Brisket. Horrifyingly I have now lived long enough to see these cuts that I was always wary of in the first place when they featured in the kitchens of the working class, appear on upmarket restaurant menus alongside very fancy prices. As most of the current customer base has no former memory of them they are greeted with Oohs and Aahs of delight. Being still a rather fussy eater I avoid them if I can. Meals I was in fact more keen on as a child included Liver, Kidneys, Stuffed Hearts and Sausages, most especially the latter.

In deference to our father's fervent Catholicism, on Fridays we always had Fish, even long after he had died. I found some fish meals, particularly those simmered in milk, most unappetising, mainly because Nellie had never got the hang of how to thicken a sauce with flour and insisted that milk flavoured with salt and parsley was actually Parsley Sauce. She was never a confident cook, putting her lack of skill down to the fact that when she and her siblings were growing up in Maxim Road, Crayford, there was such a lack of food that our Grandmother had been totally unable to provide any kind of role model. Not that she expressed it quite in those terms of course. I definitely recall other Friday fish meals of Sprats, Kippers and Bloaters with much more enthusiasm than her attempts at simmered fish with any kind of home-made sauce. The sauces I was happiest with and accustomed to were HP, Daddy's and Tomato and when we last discussed this my brother was in full agreement, he too recalling our mother's cooking with a certain lack of enthusiasm.

Although both of us remember a tin of Fry's Cocoa suddenly appearing as a supper drink in 1949 or 1950, most children drank tea with their meals alongside the grown-ups. We were aware that as rationing decreased some school friends were occasionally allowed Tizer or Lemonade but we only managed that on those occasions when we were required to sit outside a Pub with the adults inside. Even then Old Nan grumbled and complained that it was a waste of money saying she had no time for Bleeding Brahmans demanding lemonade to Sweeten Their Piddle. On Pub occasions though she was ignored and we couldn't help but feel triumphant.

Breakfasts back then were infinitely more straightforward than they are today. There was no choice of Muesli and Yoghurt was unheard of so weekday breakfasts usually consisted of bread and jam in summer and porridge in winter. I should add that the porridge was of the rustic variety with no choice of flavourings and definitely not QuikCook. An occasional egg might be served to children on Sundays though their fathers and sometimes their mothers might have bacon as well occasionally. I envied Molly and Georgie a door or two down whose mother regularly provided Shredded Wheat but when I suggested we follow suit I was told boxed cereals were much too dear, like cube sugar which Bernard had a longing for and we occasionally also saw at their house. Old Nan said in her experience it was only Nobs and Toffs who went in for Frills such as cube sugar and it was likely such people went in for Real Cream as well. This remark caused me even more confusion because I thought Cream was the Libby's Milk that we regularly poured over our tinned pineapple at Sunday teatime after consuming the compulsory two slices of bread and butter. The idea that there was something else known as Real Cream was astonishing.

Libby's Milk was sometimes served alongside the Sunday tea-time trifles our mother learned to make from Woman Magazine in the doctor's waiting room. Her first attempt appeared in 1953 in honour of my brother turning six, not exactly a Birthday Party like some children were beginning to have in those post-war years, but all the same a most Special Tea. A Swiss Roll from the Co-op had been sliced and arranged at the bottom of a glass bowl, topped with a can of Fruit Salad and set with an orange flavoured jelly. This was left to completely solidify in our always chilly Front Room and when Bernard returned from school at 3.30 it was ready to be first admired and then eaten. His excitement was palpable and increased when the can of Libby's appeared. He told me it was just like Sunday Tea Time and his ears turned pink with delight when we sang Happy Birthday. He still remembered the occasion when we spoke of it at Cape Wrath in the year before he died.

Other infrequent treats were Lyons Fruit Pies, appearing on our tea table intermittently, never a whole one each, and cut carefully in half for my brother and me to share and occasionally into three pieces when our mother sampled the smallest piece. It only occurred to me recently that she rarely appeared to partake of these occasional treats and I imagine that could only be because of the cost. An annual delight that all of us did take part in was the making and eating of the pancakes on Shrove Tuesday, served deliciously with the juice of a lemon and a sprinkling of sugar and our mother enjoying them just as much as we did. Other festive food included hot cross buns appearing without fail in time for Easter, though we never made our own, and by 1953 usually we were also given a chocolate egg like every other child in the street except ours would be considerably smaller than most.

Throughout our childhood there were some foods that were completely free such as Hop Tops, Cobnuts, Chestnuts, Blackberries and Crab Apples and if you could face it, Hedgehogs. But you had to make the effort to collect them which of course we did with enthusiasm except for the Hedgehogs which were usually left to our Grandmother who was more resilient about the fate of small mammals. There were also foods that were purloined on a seasonal basis from local farmers such as Apples, Pears, Cherries, Peas, Beans and New Potatoes and we viewed these thefts less as pilfering and more as a Right passed down via the generations before us.

Bernard enjoyed the trips into the surrounding countryside probably more than I did because it gave him a splendid opportunity for more in-depth bird watching than was immediately at hand in the grimy environs of York Road, even taking into account the local chalk pits. The family dog, who had safely avoided contracting TB, was also usually enthusiastic until he became older and incapacitated by a form of canine arthritis which refused to respond to the usual treatments.

Several years ago looking back over those years between the mid-1940s and the mid-1950s we both came to realise that there were a number of typical Kentish dishes that we never came across. No member of our large extended family seemed to make, have any interest in making or the necessary knowledge as to how to make local delights such as Gypsy Tart, Kentish Pudding Pie, Cherry Batter Pudding or Lenten Pie. Others spring to mind also, but they all remained a mystery to us and I only tried them decades later as an adult with the assistance of a suitable cookery book. If she was still alive, Old Nan would undoubtedly say that this was because they were foods that only Toffs & Nobs ate but somehow I don't believe that.

## One of Them There Aphrodites

It was Old Nan who first described Auntie Queenie as One of Them There Aphrodites and because my teacher, Mr Clark at St Botolph's had recently introduced our class to the Myths of Greece and Rome I knew at once that she was referring to the daughter of Zeus who was an important figure as far as the Greeks were concerned. My father had told me a great deal about his time in Greece when touring Europe during World War Two, including the promise that we would all go there one day for a holiday so I listened very carefully to the conversation that was going on between my Grandmother and several of the Aunts but found it confusing. This was perhaps not surprising as it concerned matters transgender, a subject I was not familiar with. Matters transgender were likely to confuse even the most open-minded back then of course and you couldn't really describe anyone in our immediate family as open-minded.

Everything concerning the topic is a lot more straightforward these days and there even seems to be a growing delight and satisfaction in the burgeoning publicity surrounding it. This must be more than rewarding for those immediately involved in defining sexual category on a regular basis, a definite step forward. On local radio, excited discussions frequently emerge on the possible complications regarding such issues as Gender Neutral toilets, particularly in schools where it appears that mounting numbers of under tens are now in the throes of personal discussion around whether they are male or female and what their preference might be. Thoroughly modern up-to-date parents appear to take this process of decision making in their stride, insisting that the choice has to be made by the six-year-old him/herself and displaying to one and all that they are completely at peace with what would certainly have been a very unusual and disturbing problem sixty or seventy years ago. Had I been thrust into such a situation as a primary age child I would have found it quite thrilling to choose a new name, which in my case might well have been Sebastian should I choose to become a boy and I would have even contemplated Aphrodite as a splendid choice for any boy considering change although my favourite girl's name at that stage was Suzanne. I cannot imagine my parents being at ease with this particular dilemma on any level whatsoever.

In those first few years after the War, we like scores of other families around us were certainly not in any danger of becoming progressive thinkers particularly where matters associated with sex and gender were concerned. Accepting the customary developments and practices alongside being male or female was hard enough – to add a further dimension was simply out of the question. To harbour someone within your immediate family who was afflicted with a problem relating to sexual identity of any description was a horror hard to imagine and discussion around the subject was inclined to be insufferably shameful rather than simply awkward. There was therefore no open debate and very little closed debate concerning those among us who might ultimately turn out to identify simply as Gay or

Lesbian which must have made some lives within the community harder than they really needed to be. We children were all expected to conform to standard norms in every way, playing together in amorphous groups, boys mostly with boys and girls mostly with girls. Although some girls were indulgently allowed to be Tomboys, boys who were clearly a great deal more comfortable playing with the girls rather than boys were often frowned upon, tut tutted about and given footballs and motor cycle magazines for Christmas. It was also anticipated that we would each of us make one or two Best Friends with whom confidences could be shared and of whom our parents would largely approve and those who failed to attract Best Friends were a disappointment and might even be castigated for social failure.

The parameters around community acceptance as far as adults were concerned were even more stringent. Little wonder that poor Auntie Queenie of Stonebridge Road set tongues wagging so violently. She seemed destined to always cause a stir wherever she went. As the Aunts all agreed, however, you could never rely on her to keep her head down. I never quite knew how she was related to us because she wasn't a subject that anyone cared to speak of in any depth but she was definitely a relative from my mother's side of the family because at one time Aunts Mag, Martha, Maud, Rose and Freda were all more than familiar with her and when her name was mentioned they each sniffed a bit and tried to change the subject – even Freda. She always seemed to be quite an old lady to Bernard and me, but decidedly eccentric and with Attitude which of course would be one of the reasons why our grandmother disliked her so much.

She had lived in Crayford at one time but left because of some social misdemeanour which took place when she was working at Vickers and which had embarrassed my uncles so much. I was never clear about what it actually was but her leaving caused Old Nan to loudly proclaim that The Day That Dirty Doxie Left Was A Day For A Knees Up. She moved quite close to us to a couple of upstairs rooms in the house that took in long term lodgers on Stonebridge Road, Northfleet where one of her neighbours she was proud to relate was Young Arthur Greenslade who ultimately became a famous pianist and conductor. She had actually spoken with both him and his mother several times. Aunt Mag said they would have crossed the road to avoid her if they had Known Anything about her. But she only said that later of course. Nellie agreed adding that People Like Queenie ought to be kept away from normal folk and her roaming all over the place just however she liked wasn't right at all, not by anybody's standards.

Meeting her outside the Northfleet Council Offices one afternoon though she pretended to be pleased to see her and asked why she'd decided to come to Northfleet and Queenie lit a fresh cigarette and waved it in the air, pursing very red lips and saying she wanted to be close to Huggens College because she'd had her name down for a while now. Our mother generally pretended to be delighted when she came across Queenie but I knew it was all an act because if she dropped by our place, we would more than likely be told to be very quiet because we were going to pretend we were not at home. This was a bit of a risk when my brother was very small as the idea of us all hiding under the kitchen table and the accompanying silence invariably made him cry quite loudly. Then Queenie would call out and rap on the windows and would eventually have to be let inside which was embarrassing. As far as Huggens College was concerned Aunt Martha said they'd never let the likes of her through the gates because places like that were for the Toffs and everybody knew that. I asked if Auntie Queenie was a Toff but I was ignored.

 She always designed and made her own Outfits because she said she had always been Fussy about clothes and the garments she wore were so colourful and adorned with so many beads and trailing pieces of silk and chiffon, she often managed to look as if she had stepped out of the Chatham Empire Christmas Pantomime. When she was younger she had even been on The Halls dressed as a man and singing songs like Burlington Bertie which Old Nan said suited her down to the ground. This was puzzling because my grandmother had done a fair bit of singing for money herself when she'd had a skinful though she stuck more to cinema queues and pubs on a Saturday night. Auntie Queenie wore exotic hats with veils attached over her very long and very red hair that my mother said was Not Natural, making it sound like an adjunct to her unfortunate Condition because on the occasions when she came under the scrutiny of whispered discussion she was always described first and foremost as Not Natural. Old Nan said she was Dyed Up to the Eyeballs and always maintained that the basic problem was most likely due to something that had Happened to her poor mother when she was Carrying but wouldn't go further than that because she'd never been one to gossip. But then Old Nan was given to saying a lot of things that turned out not to be completely accurate.

Whatever it was that so sadly divided Queenie from the rest of the family and couldn't be spoken of, we children were absolutely certain of one thing. We must never, ever go Into a Lavatory with her. Until the moment I was given this particular directive it had never occurred to me to do so but of course from then on I was driven to distraction by curiosity as were all my female cousins except Margaret who was older and sensible and about to get a job in Dolcis in Dartford. On an afternoon visit to our place with her mother my cousin Pat wanted to know what she should do if she was Busting To Go and was told to Just Bust which was of course disappointing. Aunt Martha related, in a suitably low voice, to my mother that she had been forced into that very position on Gravesend Prom one Sunday afternoon, coming across Queenie out of the blue who she was sure had Had One Or Two. Anyhow, whether she had or not, after two cups of tea from that fella who ran the tea-stand with the striped awning, where they sold iced buns as well, they were both of them Busting. Like it or not she found herself inside the Public Conveniences with Queenie who was Bold as Brass about it. Wouldn't you think that she would have more idea of what was decent? More consideration for others, for Normal People, but No – Not Her!

Pat and I exchanged Looks whilst my mother commiserated and said she would have been all of a fluster if it had been her and wouldn't have known where to put herself and that Queenie had always been Known for being a Brazen Cow which given her situation could only make you Wonder. She reminded Martha that their only brother, our Uncle Edgar had come across her actually Piddling up against a wall at the bottom of Harmer Street one Friday night and he could always be relied upon; he'd rarely been known to tell a lie. After all, he'd been at Dunkirk hadn't he? That statement was not exactly true of course because during the War he had not left the boundaries of Crayford and kept a very low profile due to his birth never having been registered. They did agree though that when it came to being Bold as Brass and Brazen, Queenie was right there at the front of the queue. Never forget there'd been that airman she'd met out Shears Green way at the Battle of Britain when it first opened, the Poor Bugger she'd led up the garden path with all her talk of going to live in Swanscombe. Look where that got her. He'd had the wool pulled over his eyes good and proper hadn't he? My mother poured more tea and said it fairly made her hair stand on end just to think about it; in fact it didn't bear thinking about at all.

When the Aunt and Cousin had been despatched on the bus back to Iron Mill Lane, Crayford, and I had gone back to my Circus colouring book because it always paid to be half engaged in something inoffensive when asking questions on matters that might be deemed offensive, I asked my mother, now occupied with washing up, what made Auntie Queenie Bold as Brass when going into the Public Lavatory with Aunt Martha. But the only reply I got was that I had Big Ears and should not be listening to things that didn't concern me and I would feel the back of her hand if I wasn't careful. So I stopped because the back of her hand could be painful. However, the next time a Family Day Out to Southend was suggested I was most enthusiastic. A Day Out was in itself something of a treat particularly as we would undoubtedly at some stage find ourselves at The Kursaal where more than likely we would come across Auntie Queenie herself selling candy floss or raffle tickets which she often did at fun fairs and circuses. Aunt Mag said this was because nobody in their right mind who ran a proper business would give the likes of her a job and you couldn't blame them could you? Old Nan said that it was because she was a Bleeding Freak Show in herself but because we were standing waiting for the Tilbury ferry at the time, her daughters quelled her with hostile looks which wasn't easy because she was not known for being easily quelled. Later on she insisted it was no exaggeration and May the Lord Strike Her Dead if she was telling a lie and that even the Hospital up in London had taken photos of her Down Below, regular as clockwork, year in and year out and had told her she was One of Them There Aphrodites which meant she was Not Normal. I listened to all of this with the greatest interest whilst pretending to examine a poster extolling the virtues of a Day at Southend on Sea. I was very curious as to the precise details of that which made an Aphrodite so excitingly abnormal. I thought it most unlikely that Zeus had been in any way involved.

It was a bitterly cold Spring day when our ungainly family group comprising of Old Nan, all the Aunts, most of the cousins and even several Uncles either on Shift Work or Out Of Work emerged from the station. Our father was leading the way because his love of fun fairs was especially great, my brother sitting on his shoulders and loving being carried so high above the rest of us. First of all we had to eat our picnic on the beach, huddled against the groynes in a brutal and penetrating wind and then there was a lunchtime visit to the pub so that the men and Nan could down a pint. But eventually we headed in the direction of The Kursaal, at that time quite the largest fun fair in the South of England and mid afternoon found it relatively empty with no queues for the rides. However, as afternoon turned to evening the crowds would grow thick, the laughter loud and the music deafening. The men with the teenage boys close behind headed for the shooting range, the women to the ghost train and most of the children to the roundabouts and swingboats where Auntie Queenie could be found Large as Bleeding Life according to Old Nan, and with no shame on her, dispensing Candy Floss with her coils of hair redder than ever and a big smile on her face. She seemed surprised to be immediately enveloped by an eager group of female relatives under twelve greeting her with an enthusiasm that was clearly unusual and causing her to hug each one of us hard and say how lovely it was to see us all. Our mothers, some still in the ghost train tunnels, but some hard on our heels were visibly less excited to come across her and later Old Nan claimed you could have knocked her down with a feather but that was undoubtedly an exaggeration.

As soon as we had eaten our free candy floss which Cousin June said was all very well but Auntie Queenie had made sure she gave us very small portions which went to show that she was Tight, just as our grandmother maintained, a chorus arose. We all needed to Do a Wee – and it was urgent because we were all Busting to go and did Auntie Queenie know where the Lav was and if she did could she take us? Margaret, about to have her sixteenth birthday, stared around at us coldly disapproving as Queenie rose to the occasion and ignoring protests from the mothers, collected us up like some kind of colourful Kursaal Pied Piper. We skipped along behind her in a flurry of excitement. To our great disappointment she simply directed us into separate cubicles and we did not get the slightest glimpse of her underwear which June had said would most likely differ substantially from anything our own mothers might wear and be a most unlikely colour – even perhaps black satin. Mostly our mothers wore voluminous white or peach winceyette bloomers at the time, from Gravesend market, elasticated at the knee and changed twice a week regularly.

Auntie Queenie stood waiting patiently with Little Ann and Little Violet, the last two To Go as the rest of us strained to produce trickles and by the time we re-emerged several mothers were hovering anxiously. Nellie pinched my arm hissing through clenched teeth that she had told me again and again Never Ever to go into a Lav with Auntie Queenie and why didn't I ever listen because when we got home she would make sure I was sorry. Despite all our best efforts we seemed destined never to solve the mysterious scandal closely associated with Public Conveniences that clearly revolved around Auntie Queenie though Pat and June maintained it was simply that her tits were not in the right place – they were hanging down round by her bum.

Little Violet thought that must be wrong because how did she feed her babies if her tits were not in the usual place? June said people like her never had babies anyway. Little Violet wanted to know why. Margaret said that tits being in the wrong place could happen to anybody but she wasn't going to join in the conversation any further because it Wasn't Right and we should not be discussing other people's tits in the first place. Some People, she added mysteriously were just Different and there wasn't anything that could be done about it.

I was still consumed with an insatiable curiosity. It was to be years before I would discover that our extremely exotic and undeniably eccentric Aunt, who could always be relied upon to give rise to rumour and gossip and whose real name was not Queenie at all but Victoria Eugenie Dorothea, was in fact a True Hermaphrodite and had indeed at one stage been of enormous interest to and greatly photographed by the Medical Profession. Sadly she never managed to gain entry to Huggens College but lived on in Stonebridge Road for years into the future. None of us were ever to get even a glimpse of her underwear.

# The House By The Station

Hamerton Road lay between Station Road and Railway Street and undoubtedly still does. It was a hop, skip and a jump from Northfleet Station, so close that you could feel the rush of the trains from the end of Little Nanny's back garden which was very exciting when the Express careered past headlong towards London. Little Nanny was actually our Great-great Aunt Martha Irons but we called her Little Nanny because she was very old and very little and because Bernard got muddled up with all the Greats. When I was very young I was led to believe she was my Grandfather Edgar Constant's maternal aunt and presumably she had married a Mr Irons but whatever became of him I never knew. We seemed to know very little about her apart from that and the fact that she had at one time lived in the village of Old Betsham, and we never knew when or where or for how long she lived there. But what was absolutely clear was that it was a place to which she was still very much emotionally attached, evidenced by her keen desire to go on long country walks involving that particular village.

We had a great deal to do with her when we were growing up. This might have simply been because she lived conveniently close by in Northfleet whereas our mother's other relatives all seemed to live in Crayford. She visited us regularly every Tuesday afternoon all through the war when I was still an only child, regardless of air raids and flying bombs. It would have taken more than Adolf Hitler's fun and games to deter Little Nanny from her walking routine because she had walked every day of her life and so remained upright, active and slender until the day she died.

She always counted the steps from her house to ours and although I remember them being impressive in number I now completely forget whether they registered in the thousands or tens of thousands. On Thursday mornings we usually walked to her house and then sometimes we all went together on the bus to Gravesend to buy shrimps for tea, or even a crab if my mother was feeling flush.

I liked Little Nanny although her house was rather intimidating to me when I was very young, being taller and somehow more narrow than our own, with steps beside the front door that led down to a dark and mysterious basement where the Bogeyman lived. Later I learned that a fat woman with curlers in her hair lived there and her name was Bridie so I thought she might be married to the Bogeyman or even perhaps his mother. You entered the house directly into the front room just like ours but in Hamerton Road it was always called The Parlour and nobody ever sat in it not even at Christmas. My mother said you would take the Devil by the horns to light a fire in the grate because the chimney had not been swept for nigh on forty years. By contrast our chimney was swept regularly. The Parlour held a great deal of soft furniture covered by dust sheets and several sideboards and display cabinets. The sideboard tops were crammed with glass domes under which were a number of stuffed birds and animals. I remember a squirrel and an owl that I tentatively and unimaginatively named Nutkin and

Owley. Bernard was, predictably perhaps bearing in mind his later passions, quite mesmerised by an alarmingly lifelike hawk. As he grew older and his ornithological knowledge deepened, he informed me it was a Kestrel, a fact that did not interest me. It was a species he was later to have a close association with, rather astonishingly keeping one in his son's bedroom in Chatham in the late 1960s, assuring anyone foolish enough to express bewilderment that the bird was necessary Company for the two year old. This was the bird that on one memorable occasion I was persuaded to care for against my will for several weeks whilst he chased Golden Eagles in the North of Scotland. But in the late 1940s he merely stood before it, confined within glass, a look of wonder on his face.

The Hamerton Road glass fronted cabinets were home to various china keepsakes from long ago trips to Margate and Ramsgate as well as a grand collection of Bristol Glass Jars that were said to be Worth a Bob or Two. These items vied with each other for space and were too many for me to count. When my mother was given the Bristol Glass a couple of the aunts sniffed a bit and commented that they had always been of the opinion that the glassware had by rights been due to Old Nan in the first place and it had been a Mystery as to how Old Aunt Martha ever came into possession of it.

It gradually became clear to me that although Great-great Aunt Martha seemed fond of me and my brother and certainly my mother she was singularly unimpressed with others in the family, most particularly my Grandmother, and my mother's youngest sister Freda. Although I knew I was never to address Freda as Aunt because she didn't deserve any respect, sometimes of course I forgot and then my mother would close her mouth tightly and slightly shake her head in my direction. Those like Little Nanny who shared my mother's lack of approbation helped me to remember. Freda did not deserve respect because of her habit of selling non-existent silk stocking during the war and causing my mother never to be able to hold her head up in Northfleet again, or at least for a very long time. The other reason that Freda deserved no respect was to emerge years later when to everyone's surprise she unexpectedly gave birth to Baby Susan. Even Old Nan was very nearly Knocked Down by a Feather when that happened. Freda seemed quite pleased with her infant daughter, visiting all and sundry to display her and later on collecting knitted matinee jackets and bootees from everyone.

 Little Nanny never called my mother Nell, like everyone else. It was always Dearest Nellie and sometimes even Dearest Helen. Somehow we learned that this was because she had been brought up Properly and knew how to Behave. She always presented her four o'clock afternoon teas Properly. Her jam was put into a little china bowl and you helped yourself with a silver spoon which I never quite got the hang of. As for Bernard, my mother always did it for him. Her bread was always thinly sliced and sometimes she made rock cakes that were never like my mother's whose version always tasted like rocks, or as my cousin Des said, like ship's biscuits. Little Nanny's were soft and crumbly and the sultanas were plump and flavoursome. She poured my tea into a miniature china cup with a design of cherubs that she said were hand painted and when I grew older the cup passed to Bernard. I was tempted to name the cherubs but couldn't think of anything holy enough.

She always wore black dresses down to the floor and white caps with a lace trim. Her winter coat was black too with a Persian Lamb collar that Old Nan said was probably full of moth and she wouldn't give it house room herself because she had never held with Persian Lamb. She held with Beaver though and once my grandfather had bought her a full length beaver coat with his winnings at Crayford Dogs. My cousin June told me that it was bought second hand and didn't really count. Generally speaking Old Nan was not welcome in the Hamerton Road house for reasons that were never actually spelled out but had something to do with my grandfather scraping the bottom of a barrel which just had to be endured because not much could be done about it now and after all She was the mother of his Poor Children.

Little Nanny could remember things from back in history like when Rosherville had one of the most popular pleasure gardens in the country that had been open to the public for more than seventy years. My closest brush with Rosherville was on the interminable walks back from Gravesend and the presence of a pleasure garden, which I was told was a kind of a fun fair for grown-ups would have made the walk much more bearable had I only known about it at the time. When she had been the same age as me families visited the gardens for the day, even coming down from London on steamers, and because the entrance fee was so high, they brought picnics with them and ate them whilst watching tightrope walkers and firework displays and even a dancing bear at one time. The Gardens had been a magical place back then. I once asked Old Nan if she remembered The Gardens with the dancing bear and she said it had always been a dead and alive hole and could get very rough at times. Little Nanny said that was on account of them letting The Likes of Her inside the gates. It seemed better not to delve into this difference of opinion too deeply and so it was left at that.

As I grew older and Little Nanny's sight diminished I was detailed to visit her after school once a week to thread needles, always with robust lengths of black thread because her pastime when she wasn't walking was sewing. She also sewed with an old fashioned machine which she said was going to be left to me When she Went. I wasn't terribly keen on sewing myself, however, so this promise did not make quite the impression it should have done. However my brother was excitedly anticipating what was to be Left to him – the stuffed animals and birds, the Kestrel in particular.

The old lady and my mother grew even closer over the years and it was at the Hamerton Road house during afternoon tea that sometimes a great many tears would be shed after the war when my parents' relationship began to deteriorate. My mother would talk about how she dreaded getting onto a bus for fear of coming across one of his Fancy Pieces and that they were as Bold as Brass and Great-great Aunt Martha would commiserate and say that she would light candles on Sunday though that didn't seem to help much at all. She also spoke of wanting Dear Nellie to move into the Hamerton Road house when she Went and my mother always told her that would be lovely, nothing could be better but later commented to our father that she was perfectly happy at 28 York Road. This was because after all these years the agents for the landlord, Messrs Porter, Putt & Fletcher, knew her and had her down as Reliable. It would not be easy to start again with perhaps a different agent.

The woman called Bridie who lived in the basement with the Bogeyman was also reliable and Little Nanny said she was always prompt with her five shillings a week rent. This was because she was on to a Good Thing for two rooms, a scullery and a share of the outside lavatory and knew which side her Bread was Buttered on. When I stopped believing in things like Tooth Fairies and Bogeymen I learned that Bridie had abandoned her husband who knocked her about when he came back from The Leather Bottle and for the low rent she also cleaned the upstairs rooms occupied by her elderly landlady. Nobody seemed to think she did a very good job with the cleaning but then when you get older and eyesight fails people like Bridie who was a Smarmy Cow are likely to Take Advantage.

For years Bridie Kept Herself to Herself but as Little Nanny grew more frail she seemed to become rather more assertive and at times even hostile. When I visited after school with Molly one day to thread needles she met us at the front door and told us to Clear Off because the Poor Old Soul was sleeping. We did clear off but I was then nearly thirteen years old and uneasy about it. My mother visibly bridled when I told her and said she had never trusted that Two Faced Cow and first thing Monday morning she would go round there and Clean Her Rotten. If she actually did so is debatable because

Nellie was always a master at blustering but not so good at backing up her indignation with anything concrete. A week or two later at the age of ninety four, Great-great Aunt Martha died and there was continuing drama because somehow or other Bridie failed to put a notice in the paper and it was only by chance the relatives found out where and when the funeral was to be. But then to be fair these occasional lapses of memory and indifference with regard to the organisation of funerals were to plague our family through more than one generation. When Little Nanny died Freda said the lack of information was most likely because grief does terrible things to people. My mother said that Freda talked a lot of tripe and tommy rot and to ignore her.

Although over the years my grandmother and aunts had had little to do with Martha Irons, she was Family after all and they were collectively outraged. Aunts Maud, Mag and Martha spoke for months afterwards about it and maintained that considering how Bridie had benefitted it wouldn't have been much to ask for a notice to be put in The Gravesend & Dartford Reporter or, considering the Poor Old Dear's association with the village of Old Betsham, even The Kent Messenger. It would have given them the opportunity to arrange a Proper Send Off. You could have Knocked Old Nan for Six when she found there was only tea at the Wake once it had been hastily organised and not a solitary drop of Gin. Aunt Mag said quite sensibly that maybe we should thank the Lord there was a Wake at all although she did think that Nell, being the Favourite after all, should have made it her business to find out What Was What. But my mother was bewildered and kept wondering why Bridie never handed over the Victorian sewing machine that had been promised to me. However, she took comfort from the fact that the wind would soon be taken out of that Brazen Cow's sails when she was thrown out on her ear. But that did not actually happen because of an astonishing development. Somehow or other and Old Nan could never for the life of her fathom why Nobody Had Twigged, it had escaped our collective notice that far from being the tenant of the house in Hamerton Road, Great-great Aunt Martha appeared to be the owner. In a sudden Will made several months before she died she passed it on to Dearest Bridie Who Had Always Been Such a Support & Comfort. But of course coming from a family unfamiliar with the making of Wills, we were completely unprepared for what had eventuated. Later on our Waterdales Uncle Walter said that Wills were a complicated business but could be Challenged though the challenging of them was an expensive undertaking and perhaps it was best not to go down that Path.

Losing possible ownership of a house at a time when few People Like Us could have dreamed of home ownership was not a good development. We knew that because so many family members said so and although our mother thought that the opinions of many of them were Not Much Cop, she did listen to Uncle Walter. That was probably because he was not only a foreman at the Paper Mills but also involved in The Union. Nevertheless she was strangely pragmatic about the whole business and when we were to discuss the event in the early years of the twenty-first century Bernard said it was because she had been too naïve to absorb the information and that primarily the fault lay with Great-

great Aunt Martha who had foolishly allowed herself to be duped. It was essential, he said, to be Precise when writing a Will, and not allow others, to influence your basic wishes. Such a situation would not be allowed to occur with his own Will making, he would make sure of it.

Strangely it had been the loss of the Victorian sewing machine rather than the house in Hamerton Road that had caused our mother most distress. For Bernard it had been the greatly desired and admired Kestrel under the glass dome. Our cousin Des said that more than likely both these items had been considered Junk and had ended up in the Friday dust cart collection.

## Long Gone Pub Sounds

When we were growing up in our little corner of North Kent there seemed to be a pub on every corner and, unlike today, each was definitely flourishing. Although neither of our parents could have ever been described as dedicated drinkers, they nevertheless seemed to spend a great deal of time on Licensed Premises. Some places had what were called Children's Rooms where under-eighteens were allowed to sip on orange juice or lemonade and flick through filthy piles of fly-ridden comics. If no such facility was available we simply hung around outside which was infinitely more lively even though I was invariably in charge of my brother, usually safely belted into his pushchair. Our mother always proclaimed loudly that she could not abide alcohol and told terrifying and possibly exaggerated stories about her own parents' drunkenness which, if they were all to be believed, should have resulted in neither she nor her siblings reaching adulthood. Later of course, Bernard learned that a couple of them had indeed possibly died during drunken mishaps.

We had favourite pubs where we as a small family group ventured on a regular basis but when visitors in the form of aunts, grandmother and numerous cousins descended we spread our patronage far and wide. I dimly remember The Black Eagle in Galley Hill Road near Swanscombe where my cousin Pat and I played hopscotch on the pavement and fought over a packet of crisps. That very same evening I seem to remember us moving on to The Plough in Stonebridge Road, or was it The Ingress Tavern? Some ten years ago The Plough still appeared to be open if memory serves me correctly. My brother has no memory at all of these places. There were pubs aplenty in Northfleet High Street during those post war years – The Railway Tavern and the Edinburgh Castle being our most favoured with The Huggens Arms in nearby Creek Road, and The Rose in Wood Street coming a close second. Old Nan told a tale or two about a place she remembered from years past called The Blue Anchor that even then no longer seemed to exist and added that even if it did she would never set foot inside the place and we assumed that she had at some time been unceremoniously ejected. Neither would she set foot inside The Little Wonder at 78 The High Street so presumably there was a story to be told there too. Our older cousin Margaret liked to go to the Marquis of Granby or The Coach & Horses, both situated on The Hill, close by St. Botolph's church, because then we could all roam the churchyard that even then was derelict and offered all kinds of amusement. Infrequently we boldly entered The Queen's Head at number 39 The Hill though our mother maintained they were toffee-nosed in there and she didn't feel comfortable. Our father, however, cautiously expressed approval of the landlord and his family because their children were being sent to the local Roman Catholic School in Springhead Road rather than the much more conveniently closer St Botolph's where my mother determined I should go.

When our father managed to purchase his first motor bike with sidecar, an Ariel, we embarked into new and until then unfamiliar areas patronizing The Bridge Inn and The Huntsman in Dover Road East and even The Six Bells in Old Perry Street. Occasionally we went to The Fleet Tavern in Waterdales and met up with my father's oldest brother Uncle Walter and his wife, Aunt Lou. On such occasions I played sedately with my cousin Connie, and took particular care of my brother making sure he didn't cry, fearful of the wrath of this particular uncle who ruled over his large family of mostly boys in a manner that was truly terrifying. At some stage in 1947 there was great excitement when The Battle of Britain in Coldharbour Road, Shears Green opened where there was not only a children's room with lots of books to read but also a garden with swings. Some years later a local manor house appeared to be converted into the New Battle Of Britain and the old building was demolished. Decades on it seems that this iconic pub has teetered under threat of demolition once more.

On really special occasions when perhaps a wedding anniversary was to be celebrated, or Christmas was almost upon us, we self-consciously entered The Tollgate Inn on the old Roman Road, Watling Street dressed in our best with our mother trying to appear as though frequenting such upmarket places was simply a daily occurrence. Public houses, Ale Houses, Beer Halls, Taverns - in those days these were, even for teetotalers, of necessity the centre of any community. Weddings were invariably celebrated in dusty rooms above the public bars as were engagement celebrations and sometimes twenty-first birthdays. Theoretically we children were definitely banned from licensed premises but somehow or other we were all totally familiar with the convivial though slightly tense bar atmosphere, the dark polished surfaces and mirrors with gold lettering in need of cleaning, the smell of stale sweat and yesterday's spilt beer.

We never seemed to patronize any of the riverside pubs between Northfleet and Gravesend such as The India Arms, The Half Moon or The Ship all along The Shore, or The Royal Charlotte in Dock Row or The Red Lion in Crete Hall Road no matter what their interesting history might be and how enticing they might look. Later I learned that these were said to be the haunts of our father and his favourite bus conductress over some months in 1950 when his predilection for women in uniform appeared to be at its height. On one momentous occasion our mother tearfully described to Aunt Mag a distressing conversation she had overheard when joining the queue for broken biscuits at Penny, Son & Parker on The Hill. It concerned our father entertaining a certain Floozy From The Buses in The India Arms which everyone knew was a place into which No Decent Woman would venture. My aunt made sympathetic noises and a fresh pot of tea and said things about Men Being Men and that some of them were more like animals, and thank the Good Lord she had a Good One because her Harold would never stray. And later my mother remarked to another aunt that there were Things she had heard about Harold but far be it from her to spread gossip.

In the years following our father's death our mother would avert her eyes from the offending buildings along the riverside whenever we passed and she made sure we did not have to pass in their shadow very often. Nothing would have persuaded her to darken their doorsteps. Strangely, neither would she ever consent to go into any of the pubs that were closest to York Road, where we lived. Never once to my knowledge did she sample a Half of Bitter or a Milk Stout in The Brewery Tap in Dover Road or the nearby Leather Bottel despite its antiquity and history, certainly not The Dover Castle, and under no circumstances, The Prince Albert in Shepherd Street or The British Volunteer in Buckingham Road. These latter two featured large in our lives as children, however, on those Friday and Saturday evenings in summer when the crescendo of voices lustily joining in the last sing-song of the evening penetrated the upper floor of number 28 enough to make sleep impossible. There is no doubt that those far off, long-gone pub sounds somehow or other, for better or for worse, became central to the sounds of childhood for a generation of post war working class children like us.

## Remembering to Hate the Greeks

Perhaps it was partly because my brother had not been told the stories about his time in Greece that our father told me, and partly because he was younger than me, but he had only an indistinct memory of the day the Greeks came visiting. Nevertheless he knew it had been a noteworthy if inauspicious occasion by the attitudes of both our parents and the misery that followed the visit. Sitting one night in the kitchen of his house in Tydd St Mary he urged me to tell him what my own recollections were and so I did.

One Sunday afternoon in early 1949, a black taxi swung around the corner into York Road, scattering the big, rough boys like John Dyke and his cronies who were playing marbles in the gutter. The boys ran beside the car as it slowed and finally stopped outside our door, right in front of me sitting sedately on the doorstep reading a book, which was just about allowed by my mother on Sundays during her bouts of pursuing upward social mobility. There was to be no racing the streets of a Sunday just like it was any old day of the week. A car coming to our house? Surely not! Out of the taxi stepped three plump women in fur coats, impossibly high heels, and small velour hats each adorned with a feather and a veil. Two were old like my mother and the fattest one was very old like my grandmother. They shrieked at each other in a foreign language as the driver was paid dramatically, with a white five-pound note, the first I had ever seen, and much fuss was made about the change being handed over in a plethora of notes. Then they checked the numbers on the doors either side of our house, now surrounded by the interested group of boys who had somehow been joined by a couple of mothers in Sunday aprons who tried to look nonchalant without much success.

I kept my eyes as far as possible on *The Further Adventures Of Worzel Gummidge* whilst paying great attention to their shoes. A pair of puffy ankles in silk stockings wobbled towards me and I was tapped smartly on the head by a hand laden down with rings. Her nails were an unseemly length and colour for her age. My grandmother never grew her nails and my mother's were bitten to the bone.

'And you must be dear little Jean....' My name came out all wrong from her mouth and sounded more like John. A wonderful aroma pervaded the air around her; this old lady was so impossibly glamorous I was struck dumb and could only nod but by that time my mother had appeared on the doorstep behind me with 'I think you must have come to the wrong place – who are you looking for?'

They told her they were looking for 'dear Bernard' and as Nellie tried to narrow the door space, my father also appeared and then all three of them threw themselves forward and covered him with kisses. I had never seen such a public display of emotion and could only gawp, my mouth open. Later my mother was to describe this scene as disgusting and maintain that their behaviour Turned her Stomach but at the time she, like me, simply stood and stared. By this time the three women were inside our front room, now suddenly made smaller by the sheer volume of their combined furs and the pervasive fragrance emanating from them was stronger than ever. Inside our house! Strangers simply did not come inside our house and tread all over our mats. Only family and the occasional close acquaintance were ever allowed over the threshold because if there was one thing our mother could not abide it was strangers treading on mats. Strangers were therefore kept firmly on the doorstep but somehow or other these three alien women – foreigners to boot – were actually inside our front room. The older one by now had settled herself on the arm of the sofa with a kind of thud, her fur coat opening at the front to reveal a plump stomach covered by a shiny red frock that seemed to me so beautiful it could have been a bridesmaid's outfit made for a very stylish wedding.

At some stage in the next few minutes my mother ushered me upstairs, pulled my grey skirt and pullover off me and out of the wardrobe came the lemon cotton summer dress recently bought at Gravesend Market that was supposed to be saved for going to church and for visiting. I was hastily re-dressed – clean white socks, hair brushed. She fluffed up her own hair, dabbed some Velouty for Beauty on her cheeks and pushed me downstairs again. The three women were still in the front room, now all seated with coats off, hats still on, the younger two also garbed in bright silk and adorned with strings of glittering beads. They perched on our drab and dreary 1930s three-piece suite picked up from the Dartford Second Hand Furniture Mart, with easy assurance like a clutch of exotic birds, filling the room with an unfamiliar thrill of excitement. I began to observe them with growing enthusiasm, already rehearsing the stories I was going to tell the girls at school about their impossibly glamorous lives. My father had recovered his composure and was talking animatedly. My mother's mouth was set at a grim angle. One of the younger women hugged me and told me I was a beautiful little girl and greatly heartened by this I asked her if she thought my new dress was pretty and added that I was wearing it because she was a very special visitor. My mother pinched my thigh painfully as I said this and told me to speak when I was spoken to and not to interrupt grown-up conversation. The woman who my father said was my new Aunt Philomena, told me that my dress was very lovely and she was humbled that I should wear it in her honour, and that of her sister (my new Aunt Mariella) and her mother who was not an aunt but a Madame Something Very Foreign. I became much more chatty at this stage and told my new aunts that they were wearing the most beautiful dresses I had ever seen (except at weddings) and they must have come from shops where things were very dear and they all laughed and again said how truly sweet and clever I was. I liked this very much.

My mother then called me into the scullery to help her make the tea and hissed: '…you just button your lip for once or I'll give you what for after they've gone!' So I reluctantly buttoned my lip and with very bad grace because there were so many questions I wanted to ask. Who were these extraordinary women and how could it be that they knew my father so well? Just how did he get to be on such obviously good terms with foreigners who dressed in silks and furs and paid their bills with five-pound notes? Later in the afternoon I was sent across to the corner shop because they were the only people for miles around with a telephone, to ask them to telephone for a taxi to take us all into Gravesend to the Nelson Hotel where they were staying and where we were all going to have a cooked tea! Only my brother was to be left behind, with Mr. and Mrs. Bassent next door and when he heard this of course he began to cry very loudly indeed. Aunt Mariella then decided it would be too..oo..oo croo..oo..el to leave him behind and he should be allowed to come too. Bernard cheered up immediately and was then swiftly changed into his best romper suit and blue knitted cardigan.

At the shop they were very interested. Who were the three ladies? How did they know our Dad? Were they friends of our Mum as well or just our Dad? Did they write and tell us they were coming to visit or was it a lovely surprise? I was thrilled to provide information that was later to incense my mother and truly make her Blood Boil. I happily told them that the three ladies came from a country called Greece and that they were our new aunts, that they met my Daddy during the war and they were Daddy's friends – not Mummy's. Oh and their visit was a lovely, lovely surprise.

For the very first time in my life I was going to ride in a motor car, a huge black shiny taxi that had to make two trips to get us all to the hotel. The old lady with many dramatic gestures insisted on paying for it. The excitement mounted as we sat in the hotel lobby whilst one of the new aunts negotiated a table in the restaurant for us all and a chair with a booster cushion for me and a proper high chair for my brother. My mother, by now changed into her Sunday-best black taffeta dress, also worn for funerals, her black Cuban heeled shoes and wearing crystal beads, looked more and more miserable. My father in his demob suit looked somewhat overconfident and strutted a little, saying he had heard the food at the Nelson was extremely good, to which she responded in a loud stage whisper that she wasn't hungry and anyway her stomach was churning and she wouldn't be able to keep a thing down so to tell them not to waste their money on her.

The restaurant was quite the most dazzling place I had ever been inside with tapestry wallpaper and glass chandeliers and a very sombre atmosphere. The narrow tables were covered in starched linen cloths and each place was set with a considerable amount of heavy silverware. There were napkins rolled up and secured with silver bracelets. I had never seen such glamour before and I was entranced. I was allowed to choose what I was going to eat and was urged to choose chicken because it was very special and only normally eaten at Christmas time. Then I ate something called a Peach Melba which came in a tall glass filled with tinned peaches and ice cream covered in a delicious jam sauce. A bottle of wine somehow appeared on the table which the foreign women shared. My mother only drank lemonade and my father ordered beer. Poor Nellie looked more uncomfortable than ever and sat mostly in silence eating very little. After a while the new aunts stopped trying to draw her into the conversation and instead reminisced with my father about things that had happened during the war when he had apparently, been great friends with them. Sometimes they spoke in their own language – and sometimes even my father spoke some of this strange language! They began to bring photographs out of their lizard-skin handbags and these were scrutinised with care over cups of Nescafe coffee. There was a lot of laughter and as it grew dark and the evening drew to a close, there was also a great deal of kissing and hugging and tears from the younger women.

We did not go home in a taxi. We waited for the 496 bus and while we were waiting it began to rain a soft, seeping drizzle that relentlessly soaked through our Sunday best clothing. My mother kept up a non-stop diatribe in a low voice, waiting at the bus stop, on the bus, on the walk down Springhead Road, all the way home because she never thought she would live to witness the day she would be Shown Up like that. She was Shown Up in front of the whole street and she would never be able to hold her head up in York Road again. Nobody else had ever had their husband's Fancy Pieces come knocking on a Sunday. Three Fancy Pieces – not just one of them. Three tarts all dolled up in fur coats and silk stockings if you don't mind. And the way they Carried On with all that kissing and cuddling in front of people. It had well and truly turned her stomach. She'd never witnessed anything like it in all her born days as God was her Judge. The nerve of them, stepping over all her mats, sitting on all her chairs – on a Sunday too! What the neighbours must have thought she couldn't begin to imagine.

After the visit of the trio who came to be known simply as The Greeks and who never visited again, the relationship between our parents got much worse, the arguments and insults more frequent, our mother's tears more or less constant. She never had to be reminded to hate the Greeks and as the months passed I often thought about the strange new aunts in their bright shiny frocks, their high heeled shoes and the heady piquancy that wafted about them, a fragrance tantalisingly reminiscent of both bluebell woods after a violent rainstorm and heavily spiced bread pudding fresh from the oven.

The neighbours asked me about them. Old Mrs. Bassent from next door wanted to know if our Dad had heard any more from those Nice Greek friends of his. Mrs Bennett wondered when our foreign relatives were going to pay another visit. Even Mrs Troke from the shop in Shepherd Street asked if our Mum had heard any more from those Ladies who were friends of our Dad. And to each one of them I replied that we got letters from them every week and the following summer we would all be going to Greece for a long holiday at their big house.

Whether they did send letters or not I cannot recall but I do know that my mother became in the habit of deftly steaming open a fair amount of mail before resealing it and placing it in front of the mantelpiece clock. Sometimes our parents did not speak to each other for days and our father would come back from his shift to be greeted by a vacuum of quiet. His dinner would be placed before him, eaten quickly, then he would wash and change and disappear 'off for a walk' and he stopped taking me, or even the dog, with him.

Now the retelling of the details of that day in the spring of 1949 left my brother completely silent for a while. Finally he said he remembered our front room being full of women in fur coats who drank tea and waved their arms and chattered in loud voices. He could clearly recall the unusual level of merriment and our father laughing louder than anyone else and seeming very happy. He even remembered the big black taxi and the special high chair at the hotel. He thought he remembered being fed ice cream with a pink sauce, served in a tall glass dish. He recalled only a little of our mother's misery and the way she cried so often after the Greek Aunts went away again. It had been his opinion, he said, that we simply had the kind of mother who leaned towards sadness. Others had mothers who were naturally jovial, who were cheerful, fun to be with, but ours was always weighed down with the kind of melancholy and wretchedness that immediately communicated itself to us and made us constantly watchful.

After a pause I commented that it was the hopelessness of the relationship with our father that had caused much of her misery, that I remembered her as a much happier person during those war years when our only real problems seemed to have been ensuring that our ration books were kept in a safe place and doing our best to avoid sudden death at the hands of Adolph Hitler. I think he thought that these remarks were a gross exaggeration.

# The Better People of Darnley Road

Our mother started working for the Lovells early in 1952. It was still winter and the reason I remember that is because to prepare for the walk to Darnley Road to apply for the job she first had to stuff cardboard into the winter boots our father had bought at the market. They had been a Christmas present that she quite rightly commented Hadn't Lasted Five Minutes. She had told him they weren't going to be worth the twenty-five bob he paid for them but he wouldn't listen and bought them anyway. Boots were quite uncommon at that time and under normal circumstances she would have been pleased because they certainly looked sturdy and warm. It was early December and our parents were not really Speaking because of the undue attention being paid to the Tarts and Fancy Pieces on the local buses. Nowadays you would say they were estranged but back then we didn't really have estranged, we only had non-communicative combat which meant hours filled with misery and silence. The same day they shopped for the boots that fell to pieces so quickly they also bought Christmas presents for me and my brother – the Art Compendium in a smart blue box for me and the Meccano set for my brother together with a number of second-hand books from the bookstall just inside the main market building. To my delight this year they were Enid Blyton Adventures and several Chalet School stories. It mattered little to me that most of them I had already read.

Our Cousin Margaret told me on Christmas Day, after he was already dead and buried that my father always set great store by books and once he had given her one for her birthday only she forgot what it was called and what it was about. Old Nan said she could never understand why anyone would want books in the first place and she was surprised we didn't catch something from them old fly-ridden ones because it Stood to Reason. I wondered if that was why he died and I asked her if she thought he had caught something from a book but she just told me to button my lip. It was a cold and miserable Christmas what with my mother crying all the time and telling my aunts she would never forgive herself for never forgiving him. It did no good, she said, falling out over something so nonsensical as They Knew What. They seemed to Know What but I didn't Know What and wished that I did. Bernard was much more concerned with the fact that he was not to be given the Meccano set after all and that it had to wait until he got old enough to Manage it by himself. He thought he would definitely have no problem Managing but when he said that our mother began to cry again and one of my aunts whispered that his Poor Dear Father would have been proud of him.

In January the snow began to fall and our mother said she had decided to get a Little Job because what the Widows' Pension gave us would not be enough to Get By On. Aunt Martha was also a widow and said she Got By All Right but I knew because I had been told often enough, that was because she got a War Pension on account of Uncle Paddy getting drunk when celebrating the end of the War and falling off a balcony in Italy and breaking his neck. His death was said to be as a direct result of the war. You could easily Get By on a War Pension and that was the reason why my cousin Pat had hand-knitted Angora-trimmed boleros and was in danger of being Spoilt Rotten like Joan Bennett.

It had taken a great deal of courage to answer the advertisement in the Gravesend & Dartford Reporter and our mother had shown it to and discussed it with a number of neighbours and several of the aunts before summoning up the courage to call at the address in Darnley Road where the Lovells lived. One of the problems was that she had never before in her life applied for a job of any kind. Although her large and dysfunctional family had sat firmly at the very bottom of the English class system, she and her siblings had never been sent to work outside the family unit. They for the most part took work that involved all of them, largely field work, agricultural labouring and later when their father showed an entrepreneurial spirit after a win at the races, as cold fish merchants, each one of the many daughters and one son working within the family business, generally for no remuneration. She and her sisters were expected to live at home until they married when they were handed over to the responsibility of their husbands. That was simply the way it worked, a family group that without doubt nurtured an ever-pervading familial distrust of each other yet were stuck together like glue. So, as I said, applying for a job in the same manner as the rest of society required a certain amount of mettle.

Old Nan, hunched over the first roll-up of the day, said going for a Charring Job meant she needed her

Bleeding Noddle examined and Aunt Mag observed rather more sensibly that the job would surely be gone to some other silly bugger by now but she was wrong because the woman who had initially been hired had inexplicably not turned up on the first Monday. In fact Mrs Lovell had just been about to re-advertise the position, but instead she immediately offered it to my mother; Mondays, Wednesdays and Fridays each week from nine until one, for two shillings an hour, an amount of extra cash that would make life a great deal easier for us. The Lovells lived in what I thought at the time was an exceptionally upmarket and lavish home with panes of coloured glass in the front door and a grand hallway partly paved with little black and white tiles. It was in every way superior to the houses at the bottom of Iron Mill Lane, Crayford, where all my aunts now lived in homes built in the 1920s as part of an early Council estate. The aunts all had entrance halls too; spaces much coveted by me with hooks on the wall where you could hang coats and enough room for Wellington boots on the floor and in Aunt Mag's case my cousin Ann's doll's pram too. They also had inside bathrooms and none of my cousins needed to huddle into winter coats and hurry through the backyard to visit the lav after dark in winter. Until I ventured inside the Darnley Road residence of the Lovells I had thought the houses in Iron Mill Lane, conveniently close to The Three Jolly Farmers, were the epitome of social success and had decided that once I was grown up that was exactly where I wanted to live. The Lovells of Darnley Road changed all that. My mother had been working for them for over a year and was much enamoured of the family when I was allowed to accompany her to help with the spring cleaning. My job was going to be polishing the silver. Bernard, to his dismay, was to go to school as usual.

Mr Lovell was a solicitor and I was told he was a Very Clever Man and it was quite understandable that he sometimes Got the Hump because he had a lot on his mind and a great deal of responsibility what with his job and all that. There were three grown up children. One was Mr Christopher who was also a solicitor and he worked with his father but he went to work earlier so he went on a bike. There was a daughter called Miss Brenda who was a Proper Midwife and that took a lot of studying too because you were allowed to deliver babies all by yourself almost like a Doctor did. That gave me food for thought because Old Alice who for five bob came and delivered most of the babies in York Road also cleaned up and made the breakfast porridge if required to and I couldn't imagine Miss Brenda doing that. I also thought her charge out rate might be higher. When I pointed this discrepancy out I was told that Miss Brenda would be delivering the babies of Toffs and she was nothing like Old Alice whatsoever. Then there was Lawrence Lovell, the youngest who was Up At University and Very Clever though there had been a bit of a Rumpus recently because he Fell Out with his father on account of wanting to be a ballet dancer but then he did seem to be a Silly Young Bugger. He was obviously a Silly Young Bugger because one morning when his brother Mr Christopher had missed something on the BBC News, Young Lawrence had rung the BBC up on the telephone and asked them if they would mind repeating it. They took no notice of him though – well they wouldn't would they? The Falling Out over becoming a Ballet Dancer happened when they were having their dinner because Mr Lovell came home every day at dinner time only they all called it Luncheon and sometimes just Lunch. Very harsh words were spoken that day.

Three days each week my mother prepared the luncheon and had it ready by twelve fifteen and usually she cleared the dining room afterwards but Mrs. Lovell did the washing up herself most of the time and used yellow rubber gloves to save her hands. My mother was not totally enamoured of the meals she was asked to prepare and said in her opinion they were not Much Cop but the dining room itself was really lovely and I should just see the Silver, it must be Worth its Weight in Gold. So as you can imagine I was really looking forward to my cleaning job.

Mrs Lovell was a large and untidy woman with a booming voice which I could see she was attempting to moderate on my behalf so within minutes I stopped being completely terrified of her and gave her the benefit of my Learned From The BBC mode of speaking which I could tell slightly startled her. A little later in a telephone call with someone who might even have been Mr Lovell, she talked about someone being a Frightfully Funny Little Thing and Strangely Well Spoken Under the Circumstances, so I knew perfectly well she was talking about me and I was as Old Nan would undoubtedly have noted, as Pleased As Punch.

As we were engaged in the annual Spring Clean we were not going to leave at one o'clock as was usual but would stay until five, me just for one day but my mother for the whole week. She was delighted and told me it would put a Fair Few Bob More than usual in her pocket and we might even be able to manage a week in a caravan down at Swalecliffe for Easter if we were lucky because God Knows we could all Do With A Holiday after all. I fervently hoped we would not be too lucky because for various reasons revolving primarily around the behaviour of my older male cousins I detested the Swalecliffe caravan holidays. Today I sat in the back kitchen with the dining room silver on an old blanket in front of me and applied myself to vigorous cleaning and shining, determined to impress my employer who had already told me I would have two whole shillings all for myself if I did the job properly. The array of cutlery shone brilliantly by eleven am when I could hear my mother beginning to prepare the Macaroni Cheese that was going to be served for Luncheon followed by Stewed Plums. I didn't know much about Macaroni Cheese, that was clearly something Posh people ate, but I liked Stewed Plums.

Mrs Lovell, as I had both predicted and intended, was more than satisfied with my efforts when she examined the silver and she suggested that after Luncheon I should make a start on the copper ornaments on the Dining Room Mantelpiece. I readily agreed and she said that she was going to ask Mr Lovell for his approval for raising my two whole shillings to three whole shillings because I seemed to be such a Splendid Little Worker. I told her it was a pleasure to be able to help. Then she took me into the Dining Room and gave instructions as to how to lay the table with the newly gleaming cutlery which I was entirely thrilled to do and immediately began to plan how I was going to tell Molly of 31 York Road all about it, in the greatest possible detail, possibly exaggerating just a little.

The Lovell's dining room was overwhelmingly impressive with a floor that seemed to be made out of little wooden tiles which Mrs Lovell told me was called parquet, and a high ceiling almost like a church. The oval table was of what seemed to me to be of vast proportions and I counted a total of eight curved back chairs around it, each with its own dark red velour seat. I told Mrs Lovell her dining room was quite the grandest I had ever seen, and tried to make it sound as if I had seen more than one, which of course I had not. She said it was very kind of me to make such complimentary comments – she greatly appreciated them. I skipped into the kitchen to inform my mother how well I had done to lay the impressive table for Luncheon For Five, to which she replied that I had got it wrong because Miss Brenda and Young Lawrence were not home so it was only Lunch For Three so to curb my tongue because I wasn't nearly as Smart as I thought I was. Taken aback by this I referred back to Mrs Lovell, not skipping this time and in the politest BBC tones enquired if I had got the Five For Luncheon wrong on account of the missing Miss Brenda and Young Lawrence. She laughed and reassured me there would definitely be Five For Luncheon and had I completely forgotten Mrs Hendy and myself? In that moment I became so totally suffused with joy that it was like being bathed with a deep and penetrating saturation of sunlight. I was actually going to eat Luncheon! Not just Dinner like at home, but proper Luncheon and never mind if it was sometimes merely called Lunch, just like a person in a book! And not some ordinary everyday kind of Lunch either, but one in a dining room with a Parquet Floor and a very, very high ceiling just like a Church – AND with a real silver knife and fork! Who cared if it was something only posh people ate called Macaroni Cheese because I would definitely manage to force it down no matter what it tasted like. I skipped happily back to the kitchen to tell my mother just how wrong she had been.

To my abject horror she did not react well. No, no, NO, she told me in the kind of voice I knew Brooked No Argument, we would NOT be eating Luncheon in the dining room – whatever next? We would be having our Macaroni Cheese and Stewed Plums in the kitchen and I was to Button My Lip at once and not even think about answering back or giving cheek or I would be getting the Biggest Backhander of my life later on, nothing was surer than that! So to my utter misery that is what happened and we did indeed eat in the kitchen, calling it our Dinner.

Later on, walking home she said that I'd Knocked Her For Six with that nonsensical talk about eating in the dining room and why on earth did I always seem to go out of my way to bring Shame on her at every turn. Why couldn't I be like Other Girls? Like Molly Freeman or Joan Bennet or June Dawson – even Kathleen Draper or Pat Turner? All of them were a credit to their mothers but not me! I always had to stick my neck out and go one further didn't I? I always had to Argue the Toss. Nothing was ever right for me was it? If I carried on like this she would have me Put Away if it was the last thing she ever did!

I felt incensed with a combination of fury and indignation and as we got closer to home and were passing The Dover Castle in Dover Road, and she had finally stopped berating me, I firmly clutched the three silver shillings in my pocket and risked asking why it had been so wrong to want to eat Luncheon in the Dining Room because after all, we had been invited to. She looked directly at me, bracing herself into the bitter Spring wind looking suddenly tired and old. She slightly shook her head and didn't shout. She said, 'Because they aren't the same sort of people as the likes of us are they? Get that into your noddle for once. They're just a Better Sort of People than us.'

That evening I tried to tell Bernard about the Lovells turning out to be Better People than us but although he listened, rather disappointingly, he only seemed to be interested in what the Macaroni Cheese was like which I supposed was because he had not yet quite reached his fifth birthday. There were still some things he was just too young to appreciate. I assumed that as he grew older his interest in taking part in the finer aspects of life might increase. As it happened I was correct but it was to take a long time and for most of his childhood he remained preoccupied with ornithological matters.

## Walking Back From Gravesend.

Sometimes whilst my brother was still almost a baby, perhaps under two years of age, instead of taking the bus back from Gravesend, we walked and I always complained bitterly because the journey seemed overly long and mostly tedious. Before Bernard was born it was always me who was pushed in comfort in the pushchair and on those occasions we walked both ways. In those days pushchairs were less mobile than they are now and not taken onto buses unless the situation was dire because there were conductors who seemed to greatly disapprove. I was also aware that another reason for us avoiding certain bus routes might be because of the Fancy Pieces who worked on them and whom my father seemed friendly with. Whatever the reason might be, my mother largely ignored my complaints and we walked anyway if she decided so. My brother was at this time too young to understand the problems surrounding the Fancy Pieces on the buses and in any case he was quite comfortable in the push chair and usually fell asleep quite quickly.

When we almost reached the Pier Road point of The Overcliffe, my mother would point out the Northfleet Parish boundary stone and tell me to stop grizzling because now we were back in Northfleet again. I never believed her because I knew we were only entering Rosherville and that still seemed to me to be very far away from Northfleet. From time to time we stopped off in Burch Road to visit a woman who had married my uncle Arthur Steele who had previously been married to my mother's younger sister Poor Vi who like another sister, Poor Phyllis, had died in childbirth. Poor Vi had just given birth to Little Doris who, unlike Poor Phyllis's daughter Little Violet, was not forced to live with Old Nan for ever after, but was passed around the family who all had turns of her. We had two turns and as she and I did not get along at all there was a great deal of relief when she was bundled onwards to her next foster mother. Little Doris had lovely curly hair which reminded everyone of Shirley Temple and I clearly recall a game of hairdressers when some of the curls might have been cut off and I got into a great deal of Trouble. Meanwhile her father had remarried to a large and domineering woman called Edna who had an equally large and domineering daughter called Josie and a previous husband who had somehow been Lost in an Accident Before The War. My mother was very keen to persuade this new Aunt Edna to take full responsibility for the total future nurturing of Little Doris but Aunt Edna was not so keen. The problem seemed to be Her Josie who needed to be an Only Child on account of being Delicate. Old Nan said Delicate her Arse and what that Josie needed was a swift Kick up the Jacksie on account of being Spoilt Rotten and there the matter rested for the time being which I thought afterwards might have been the best outcome for Little Doris.

I knew that once, long ago, there had been a very posh hotel at the bottom of Burch Road, a proper hotel with bedrooms that you could hire and sleep in upstairs and a big room called a lounge downstairs with red carpets and a bar that sold all manner of drinks, not just gin and whisky. Our grandmother said you wore your Sunday Best to go there and that one time when she and her Edgar had won at the races they went in there on a Saturday evening and had a few. She had entertained everyone in the bar with her singing. A week later she went back and sought out the manager to tell him she would not be averse to singing for them on a regular basis but he said No, not to bother. Her Edgar had told her it was a silly idea but she wasn't good at listening to him. Her Edgar was my grandfather, dead from a heart condition and mostly a mystery to me.

I quite liked some of the buildings that we passed as we walked towards Northfleet but they could never be discussed with my brother because he was too young to notice them. There was a tall and square brick building that was the Ministry of Labour Employment Exchange and it had separate entrances for men and women so for a long time I thought it was a school for much older people, who could already read and write and knew the capitals of countries. This was simply because I knew that at St Botolph's school which I had attended since I was five, there were separate playgrounds for the boys and the girls. Near St Marks Church we came upon the typical late 1920s style shopping centre always called The Parade by my mother. There was a fish and chips shop on the corner where we sometimes bought three pennyworth of chips to sustain us on the rest of the walk and then Mrs Kean's Haberdashery where you could buy elastic and buttons and odd bits of felt and cotton. My Aunt Maud once rushed in there for a couple of pins because her knicker elastic had snapped while walking around Gravesend Market and she said that soon her drawers would be round her ankles to which Old Nan made some remark so rude that neither my mother or aunt spoke to her for the rest of the afternoon. Mr Reason the grocer was a bit further on and from time to time when feeling flush a few slices of ham would be bought for our tea, especially if one of the relatives was coming back to have their tea at our place because it was agreed that Mr Reason had the best ham in the district.

Once or twice, when accompanied by other members of the family, but never when there were just the three of us, we even paid a visit to the nearby café the name of which is long forgotten and had cups of tea from a big brown pot. Then if one of my cousins was present we would whine and nag until a plate of biscuits appeared in the middle of the table and we were told we were Greedy Little Buggers. I remember also Jo-Anne's Hairdressers close by where my Aunt Martha once had a Wave and Set causing my mother to shake her head at the extravagance of it all. Years later Pearl Banfield told me she always had her hair shampooed and set there on Saturday mornings because it was a great pity if she couldn't do that after working all week. When she got married she vowed she would continue to do so come what may.

Further on but on the other side of the road was a Post Office and a general store which we never visited but where the owner did his own deliveries on his old-fashioned bike with a large wicker basket on the front. There was also a little school badly damaged early in the war and still standing defiantly on the ridge and looking as if it had always been prepared to take on anything Hitler could dream up. It was constructed partly from flint like my future boyfriend Barrie's house in Springhead Road and it stood perilously close to the chalk pit and alongside it were a number of grand detached houses overlooking the river. I used to linger as we passed these houses, greatly admiring them and contemplating even then what kind of bathrooms they might have. My Aunt Maud said you could never tell what the insides of places like that were like and some folk who should know better were filthy in their habits. There were people living in Crayford Council Houses where the khazi wasn't fit to enter unless you held your breath. Old Nan said she didn't hold with inside khazis anyway because it Stood to Reason. She also told me I was a Right Brahman and needed to be Told. I didn't know what this meant but realised it was not complimentary.

If we were by ourselves, to keep us both amused as we got closer to home our mother would tell the same stories each time we did this walk. The house at Number 11 London Road belonged to John Lincoln the chemist who had two shops, one in Dover Road and the other in Northfleet High Street and he was a very rich man but said to be tight with his money. He was choosy she said about who he extended credit to and only showed leniency to the rich, never to the poor. In other words, she elaborated, He Wouldn't Give His Shit To The Crows! Next door to him was Dr Outred at De Warren House, he who had saved my life when I was four and was to kill my father when I was eleven. He probably later also had blood on his hands regarding the death of Mr Davis of Tooley Street because didn't he drop dead inside the chemist's shop having just come from the doctor? Though had he not had to wait so long for his prescription things might have turned out differently so there the blame could probably be shared with Mr Lincoln the Chemist.

Once we had passed De Warren House I knew that we would soon reach the house known as Fernbank that had some years previously become the first Northfleet Branch Library which my father as soon as he returned from the War insisted that I join and which afforded me information and amusement for years into the future. Fernbank for a while became the most exciting of the Grand Houses because as a borrower I had at least some limited access to it and even downstairs in the children's library I could sit and daydream about those who might have once lived there and contemplate the idea of living there myself. The room that housed the children's library at that time had once been the old dining room and the original kitchen on the same level was now a general store room. The library staff had a much smaller, cosier kitchen closer to the top of the building and beside the Chief Librarian's office.

When I told Molly about how much fun it would be to take up residence in the library she agreed immediately and suggested that we spend some time exploring the place properly on our next visit. We could do this, she said, simply by pretending to have got lost in the building should anyone challenge us. This plan worked admirably for several weeks until we were discovered one afternoon in one of the attics by the Chief Librarian herself who rarely smiled and who might have been called Miss Webster. She did not believe for a moment that we had become confused and lost. In fact she called our behaviour Unacceptable Conduct in a Public Library. Anything could have Happened apparently. One of the really Awful things that could have happened was that we might have become locked inside the building after closing time. Just imagine that! We could imagine that very well and it sounded most exciting. We could have made tea in the new and cosy little kitchen above the Adult's Section and helped ourselves to the Garibaldi biscuits. We might even have slept on the floor of the attic where we had been found and there were certainly plenty of books to read if we found ourselves not sleepy. We did not say any of this to the Chief Librarian of course and instead tried to look ashamed of the unacceptable conduct by bowing our heads and looking at the floor. Later Molly said it had been just like being sent to Mr Cook, the St Botolph's School headmaster except that Mr Cook might have caned us. The Chief Librarian's office was bigger and more impressive than Mr Cook's and she didn't cane us but instead she banned us for six weeks which was infinitely worse.

Some years later someone did get locked in the library after closing time. A young man secreted himself away in our attic and caused an enormous amount of consternation because he did so in order to kill himself. It was the Chief Librarian, she who might have been called Miss Webster, who found his body. People said she got quite a shock and had to take a few days off in order to recover.

## One or Two Canine Capers

Very nearly everyone in our corner of Northfleet kept pets, as they probably did in the rest of the town. Cats were so commonplace that they barely counted as pets because those opting not to be cat owners became host to a great many mice and maybe a few rats as well. A couple of very old ladies kept parrots that were said to be as old or in one case slightly older than they were themselves. These birds were supposedly Really Good Talkers but it was difficult to interpret their conversation. The Bassents kept a tame magpie for a while and their cat was terrified of it so later on it was given away to their daughter Ina who lived in Burch Road. They also had several smelly rabbits in cages that didn't count as pets because they were being fattened for eating. We kept hens and a rooster and they made unsatisfactory pets because they were not particularly friendly, especially the rooster, and also one by one they were eventually eaten. Our mother said that when she first moved to York Road she was lonely and so a younger brother of Poor Fred, the man she had been engaged to and ought to have married except he was Taken by the TB, gave her a gift of a linnet in a cage. The linnet sang like an angel but after a while she felt pity for it being so confined and one Sunday morning she set it free and it had flown in more and more eager and exalted circles above the street before disappearing for ever.

My brother and I were more interested in becoming dog owners than anything else and Bernard favoured one that would remain a puppy. Our mother was not all that keen and as far as she was concerned the hens and the cat served very well as family pets. During the war we had actually become dog owners briefly because Aunt Mag's next door neighbour Mrs Yates had an off-white mongrel bitch called Sally that had just given birth to a large number of puppies. At the age of three I was mesmerised by the puppies, all of them whiter than their mother and one with the sweetest little grey patch over one eye. Mrs Yates said I could definitely take that one home with me on the bus back to Northfleet making that day the best of my short life so far until my mother told me that wasn't going to happen and that in any case the puppy was much too young to leave its mother. I couldn't have cared less about that because I knew that I would make an excellent substitute mother so I executed a full scale tantrum involving throwing myself dramatically onto the cobbled path of Aunt Mag's Iron Mill Lane back yard, which was more painful than I had imagined it would be. So what happened was that the puppy was put in the bottom of a shopping bag to be taken home with us even though my grandmother said that she wouldn't give the Bloody Thing House Room if she had her way and that probably it had fleas.

I named the puppy Sugar because it was nearly as white as sugar and when we got home we gave it a saucer of milk that it knocked over instead of drinking and my mother said she wasn't surprised because hadn't she told me it was too young to leave its mother? Later on when she was safely outside hanging out washing I put the puppy on the kitchen table as gently as possible so she could eat the sugar in the basin on the tea-tray. I was sure she'd like that just as much as I did. Unfortunately at some stage the puppy fell from the table and crawled under the kitchen stove and my mother had the greatest difficulty extracting it. Some time later I learned that it had died and that it was half my fault for putting it on the table and half the fault of it being too young to leave its mother. I was quite exhausted with all the drama involved in becoming a puppy owner by this time and so felt a certain amount of relief. There were to be no more dogs at our house until my father had been back from the war for more than a year.

    I confined myself to admiring the neighbours' dogs. Pekingese were very popular at the time and Mrs Willis at No 29 had two of them called Ching and Chang. She told me they were Royal dogs and had been owned by the Kings of China and what with China being so far away, consequently they cost a fortune. My mother said she wouldn't want one even if it was going free because they dribbled and snored a lot. The Bassents at No 27 gave their granddaughter Evelyn a mixed breed puppy for her fifth birthday and its name was Doodle which was short for Doodlebug. This was because Doodle had arrived at a time when in the South East of England we were being plagued with V1 flying bombs. Joan Bennett from Buckingham Road who was constantly Spoilt Rotten was given a Labrador cross puppy at Christmas and called it Bobby. Later when Bobby unexpectedly gave birth to a litter of four his name was changed to Betsy. After the war more and more people became dog owners and some even took them for walks down to the Old Rec or out to Springhead. Most, however, did not really go in for exercise and the animals simply roamed the streets at will especially if their owners were children. This was not the case as far as the Pekingese that had cost a fortune were concerned; they stayed firmly inside their back garden and gazed disapprovingly at other canines through the slats of the garden gate.

By the time my father had returned from the war and once my brother was a few months old there was definitely talk of us owning a dog. It had always been my father's dream to have a gun dog to go out rabbiting with on the marshes, but as soon as he brought up the subject my mother predictably raised objections and reminded him that we didn't have Money to Burn and keeping a dog could work out expensive. It was when he suggested a ferret as a substitute that she shuddered a bit and relented because when she had been growing up her own brother had kept ferrets and she had never Held With Them. Shortly thereafter my father jubilantly came home with a six-month-old sleek black Labrador but my mother was still only half accepting and on hearing he had named it Susie became even more negative because she certainly didn't Hold With bitches as they without fail led to unwanted puppies. On hearing this discourse I was more and more enthused but there were sharp words and in the end my mother had her way and Susie disappeared.

The next animal was a golden spaniel bought from a breeder in Southfleet and costing several pounds and definitely male. He was a very friendly creature, licking us feverishly for the entire time he was with us which was several days. It then occurred to my parents that perhaps the intense affection, plus the fact that he seemed to bump into things a lot, meant that he couldn't see especially well and it turned out they were right. He was returned to the breeder who refunded their money with poor grace even though it appeared that the puppy was almost completely blind. There followed a hiatus in the quest to find the right dog and we confined ourselves to admiring those animals owned by our relatives. Uncles George and Harold frequented Crayford Dog Track on a regular basis and had both formed high opinions of retired racing dogs which were at the time generally given away to good homes. At one time they had two each and swore by them but my mother thought them not only unattractive but unfriendly and wouldn't consider the idea. She said the Right Dog would come along eventually.

    Aunt Martha had allowed her Pat to have a terrier cross called Rusty because he was a rusty colour. Pat told me he was almost a pure Manchester Terrier and the only thing wrong with him was that his legs were just half an inch too short to be considered a thoroughbred and that was why he'd only cost five shillings in the pet shop in Dartford. Aunt Martha added that one of his main attractions was also that he would never let another dog Be Dirty with him because he hated having anything on his back. I had absolutely no idea what she meant by this. Aunt Rose who was married to Mervyn the Welshman who was as Mean as Pigshit bought a sausage dog puppy for her Tommy and Sandra and they called it Lili after Lili Marlene because of the German connection. It sat by the fire hour after hour and its eyes and nose became singed. Tommy and Sandra soon lost interest in her but I thought she was rather beautiful.

Whilst we waited for the Coming of the Right Dog, I was allowed to keep a tortoise called Jimmy. Tortoises had suddenly appeared in local pet shops and on market stalls and cost mere shillings. They were, however, most unsatisfactory as companions and spent at least half the year hibernating in cardboard boxes full of straw. Jimmy was found to be deceased when I tried to wake him from his first hibernation and his successor, unimaginatively also called Jimmy, decided to leave us after a few weeks and we never saw him again. Molly said he had been seen ambling towards Springhead Road but although we searched he was never found.

It was after I had made several attempts to keep pet mice that the Keeshond puppy was bought from a breeder, just before Christmas 1950 and costing five pounds which was a whole week's wages. He was a delightful bundle of long silvery fur which later I would detest grooming and so it grew matted and unattractive. He was not a gun dog of course but as far as my mother was concerned at least he was male and by that time my father was simply glad to have a dog at long last. There was a great deal of discourse about what his name should be because I favoured Trixie which my father maintained was more suitable for a female. When I suggested we should use an alternative spelling such as Tricksie he was still unconvinced and said a better name would be Rex. As I had been calling him Trixie for nearly a week I thought this would cause the animal too much emotional trauma but my father was so insistent that rather surprisingly I gave in and simply called him Rexie. Unfortunately Rexie turned out to have a number of character defects, one being that he took a long time to house train and was beaten for his misdemeanours which at the age of ten moved me regularly to hysteria. Once he grew from puppyhood he began to object to going for walks, dragging on his lead as we pulled him down the Springhead Road hill towards the Old Rec and only cheering up when he knew it was time to go home again. The cause of this was never discovered but after our father died my brother and I stopped even trying to take him out for exercise and he grew fat and arthritic in the kennel our father had built for him by the outdoor lavatory. As Man's Best Friend he wasn't a spectacular example.

To Bernard, our dog, soon growing out of puppyhood, rapidly became a hazy background creature and he refocused his attention on birds. He was to become an adult before he showed a sufficient re-interest in dogs to actually want to own one. He and his first wife Janice were living in the flat above the shop in Camden Passage at The Angel, Islington when they unwisely bought a German Shepherd puppy in Petticoat Lane market and named him Romulus. He was to become a savage beast, strangely disturbed by humans who changed their shape too quickly which meant that it was unwise to go from sitting to standing position without due consideration when in his presence. Romulus was re-homed when my brother and his family moved from London to Chatham and was replaced with a Scottish Deerhound called Hereward. The Deerhound had only one fault which was to frequently mistake the local postman who at the time went about deliveries on his pushbike, for a deer. At every opportunity he would pursue him and deftly bring him off his bike by lunging at his jacket collar. This made the family unpopular and sped up their plans to relocate to a craft village in the north of Scotland where Deerhounds were to become a large feature of their lives.

My own desire to be a dog owner diminished over time and once I was in a position to make the momentous decision for myself the only future dog I was to own was a Poodle called Puddles who I never grew entirely attached to. To be fair he was not terribly fond of me either. I had more luck as a cat owner and over the next twenty years fell in love with a number of Burmese cats, each of which was reasonably self-sufficient.

## What We Read Then

There were very few books in our house when I was very young. I can remember only two - *The Home Doctor* which was immediately consulted when we developed coughs or rashes and *People of the World in Picture*s which had a disgraceful photograph of a totally naked Aboriginal family in uncivilised Australia which I was not allowed to contemplate for more than a second or two. Bernard was sure there were three books but neither of us could remember what the third one was about. When I was seven I was taken to the library by my father and became a borrower and from that moment on, hundreds of titles made their way past the front door of 28 York Road. When Molly from down the road also signed up we visited twice weekly and compared thoughts and opinions. Not coming from households where pre-schoolers were routinely introduced to bedtime stories, or stories at any time, we first of all fell upon picture books such as Helen Bannerman's Little Black Sambo series and of course the tales produced by Beatrix Potter. We very soon, however, discovered the joys of Enid Blyton starting with titles like *The Magic Faraway Tree* and progressing swiftly to the rather more sophisticated Secret Seven series. As she was so hugely prolific we stayed by Blyton's side for several years, reading and re-reading and finally advancing to the more classy and cutting edge adventure and school stories. To her credit the children's librarian made several attempts to wean us away from Enid and into a different direction but we treated her first suggestion of giving Angela Brazil a trial, with scorn. To be honest we were slightly disconcerted by the more complex sentence structure and the proliferation of what seemed like long and unfamiliar words.

When Enid Blyton became unfashionable later on and we heard murmurs that her stories were both racist and sexist we were mystified. We had never experienced the perils of Little Noddy because when he was at the zenith of his fame we were already ten or eleven years old and although the covers were tantalising, by that stage Northfleet Children's Library had developed a section for those under seven years of age, and Noddy remained out of reach inside it. We were slightly intimidated by the idea of pushing our way through the group of much smaller children and their mothers to grab Noddy from their grasp. So his sad experiences with bad golliwogs who waylaid him to steal his smart little car did not impinge upon the way we saw the world or influence our feelings towards the new immigrants from the Caribbean.

Strangely the middle-class mind sets and attitudes of the Blyton adventure story protagonists also passed us by and we found it more than easy to empathize with the characters in the books. It did not seem odd that there were often cooks and maids in the households we read about, or that large cars drove the child characters to and from the starting points of their current escapade. When Enid Blyton's heroes described a gypsy child as dirty and possibly a thief, we wholeheartedly agreed.

It was with a great deal of satisfaction that Miss Seamark, the librarian, produced Eve Garnett's *Family*

*From One End Street*, and told us that it was a milestone in children's literature. What she really meant was that it was a truly working class story and the opening sentence left the reader in no doubt about that because in an instant we learned that Mrs Ruggles was a washerwoman and her husband was a dustman. Truly a story by a middle-class author for the deserving poor, children like me and Molly! We read the book with a degree of detachment and suspicion, enjoying the struggles of the family that was so like our own but delighted to get back to the more middle-class fare we were now accustomed to.

We went on to find Richmal Crompton's William books both amusing and vastly more satisfying than anything the unfortunate Ruggles family could offer. Replete from William we threw ourselves into the Noel Streatfield sagas, *Ballet Shoes, White Boots, Curtain Up, The Circus Is Coming*, all concerning families of the one servant poor variety that we so loved. *The Children of Primrose Lane* again offered by the well-meaning Miss Seamark as a story about children like us, we enjoyed rather less because it had decidedly working-class nuances with not a daily maid or even a cleaning woman in sight. As we grew into our early teens we came across Pamela Brown's theatre stories which were thrilling because they came at a stage when we both so very much desired a successful future career in the theatre, or in Molly's case in Hollywood. Then Monica Edwards' pony books and we were once again unhindered by any problem relating to easy identification with the middle-class characters who now all owned their own steeds. Our final favourite author before we totally outgrew children's literature and progressed to Mills & Boon and magazines, was Lorna Hill who wrote enthralling stories about characters who either came from the North of England to the Sadlers Wells Ballet School or alternatively rode their ponies along the length of Hadrian's Wall and found solutions to local community problems as they did so.

And whilst we devoured these stories it would appear that the boys of the 1940s and 50s were not reading nearly as voraciously. Molly's brother Georgie, just a little younger than us, enjoyed books with plenty of pictures of planes and tanks and my own brother did not show the slightest interest in reading at all until he was tempted by Enid Blyton's *Nature Book* which contained some interesting bird illustrations. He was then further attracted by her *Book of Hedgerow Tales* but declined to progress to *The Secret Seven* or any of the Adventure series.

Everything changed, however, when he discovered Henry Williamson at the age of ten, happening upon *Tarka the Otter* in a discarded paperback edition on the upper deck of the 496 bus. From that moment he became a dedicated Henry Williamson fan, tackling each one of his books and finding out every detail of the author's life. And whilst doing so he made it his business to fully acquaint me with each detail of the man's life and work. I learned that Williamson had been born in 1895 and was an English army officer, naturalist, farmer and an accomplished writer. He won the Hawthornden Prize for literature in 1928 for *Tarka the Otter*. He had been born in Brockley, south-east London and we spent one Saturday afternoon searching for the house in which this momentous event had taken place. He had taken an active part in World War One before being gassed and returned to England.

Determined to fully understand the great man, my young brother ploughed his way through *The Patriot's Progress* and began on the fifteen volume series, *A Chronicle of Ancient Sunlight*. It was during this time that his yearning to emulate the rural life lived by his hero grew and prospered. He also voiced in an offhand way his admiration of Williamson's journey through politics, and tacit approval of the Hitler Youth Movement. Having discovered the delights of Henry Williamson it was to be years before Bernard turned his attention to another writer and the volumes that had brought so much joy to his life were always prominently displayed in his study both in Lincolnshire and at Cape Wrath alongside large numbers of ornithological works.

On my last visit to Cape Wrath Lodge I was strangely gratified to find an old and shabby copy of Enid Blyton's *Nature Book* tucked alongside the more sophisticated works.

# The Silver Lurex Jacket

Nobody had much in the way of luxuries when my brother and I were growing up. Nobody we knew at least, not even our Crayford cousins who, once our father died, seemed to be a great deal better off than we were. When I was very small there wasn't much to buy anyway so you could say it was a level playing field as far as items of clothing were concerned. In the years after the war, most children had school clothes that were passably smart and which might even be a uniform of some kind like Wendy Maxted and Margaret Snelling who both seemed to own gymslips and my mother said that was because they had Toffee Nosed mothers. We all had something rather smarter for Best or simply for Sundays, especially if we were Church Goers and a surprising number of families were. A few of the boys in particular had very shabby Saturday outfits long discarded from older brothers and were ideal for climbing up and down the chalk pits at the back of the Springhead Road houses.

None of this mattered much whilst we were under twelve, and in any case it didn't apply to every single child because there were occasional women who were superb dressmakers, and in the latter years of the 1940s could make smart Sunday two-piece outfits for their daughters out of old coats that with the addition of a simple trim, lifted the garments and their wearers to dizzy Parisian heights. Well so it seemed to me at the time. The wearers were those girls I greatly envied who wore embroidered felt bonnets to school and hand-knitted angora cardigans on Sundays. I was, as a child, inordinately impressed with angora. The ones who inspired the greatest admiration and jealousy were Rita Jenkins of Shepherd Street and Barbara Scutts of Springhead Road. To add insult to injury, and cause further envy, these two most fortunate pre-adolescents were often seen wearing shiny black patent leather shoes on special occasions.

Our own mother could and did knit and in fact she was quite enthusiastic with wool and needles. Her overall ability, however, was mediocre and she had an unfortunate habit of ignoring minor hiccups such as needle size and dropped stitches. Consequently most items produced were even to my untrained eye, largely unwearable. Decades later I was dismayed to discover she was still producing similar garments for two of my cousin Ann's young children who I could not help noticing also observed the progress of their winter sweaters with fascination and horror.

Generally speaking, like most of my school mates, I was resigned to being badly dressed. It seemed to be our lot in life. And to be fair the greater proportion of our mothers were equally poorly attired because those were the days when women seemed to be perpetually clad in shape-disguising aprons of indeterminate patterns that could be bought in British Home Stores for three shillings and sixpence apiece or in Gravesend market for two and threepence. Headscarves, tied factory-assembly-line-fashion around their heads, for the most part avoided the necessity for well-groomed hair and make-up for every day did not seem to be on the agenda although I do recall my mother occasionally dabbing Velouty For Beauty on her cheeks. A few years later curlers were worn under the headscarves giving a bulky and more awkward look that nevertheless hinted of party time ahead. For most that was not actually the case, festivities rarely came to pass and mostly the curlers simply stayed in for days on end.

By the beginning of 1952 our life of poverty and deprivation seemed to sink to a new level and I didn't need to be prompted to realise that becoming a local symbol of teenage fashion was not going to happen for me. At only five my brother was oblivious to all this and seemed proud of his hand knitted jumpers and the bib-front shorts my mother made out of my father's old tweed suit. The advent of the 1950s had coincided with a slightly elevated range of goods in the shops and on market stalls, such as somewhat frivolous rayon underwear in extraordinary colours like orange and mauve and popper beads in a range of hues that were so enticing I became consumed with a passion for owning such items. I would most definitely have resorted to organised theft had I not been so frightened of the consequences and when my cousins became old enough to regularly purloin hair slides and bottles of Evening in Paris from Woolworths I admired them but was too frightened to follow their lead.

Post-war Britain was looking brighter for most people but generally speaking life was getting worse for us. When other girls managed to persuade their mothers to buy black Ballerina Flats from Cheap & Chic Footwear in Gravesend High Street I knew better than to even ask. At that stage I had one pair of shoes, dark brown lace ups that were mended again and again by Mr Hammond in Shepherd Street until I grew out of them when they were put aside in the hope that my brother would grow into them.

Later, when I began to earn my own money, shortly before my sixteenth birthday, I headed directly into Gravesend each Saturday morning to spend it at British Home Stores and Woolworths. I thereby accumulated a quantity of Orlon cardigans in pastel shades and cotton skirts, most of which became limp and unsightly after their first wash. I was not overly concerned about quality because the ability to actually purchase an item of clothing new, at will, made me dizzy with pleasure.

Previously most of the items I wore had been passed on via cousins on both sides of the family and as the majority were girls by and large I did better than poor Bernard who got very dejected as he grew older at having to wear a succession of female jackets and raincoats with the buttons always on the Wrong Side. I had no idea how deeply this state of affairs affected him however, until a few months before his death when he revealed to me the Unhappy Tale of the Silver Lurex Jacket with the Black Velvet Collar.

Apparently he was in his third year at Colyer Road School so not exactly a new boy. He had long grown out of the school uniform passed on by a Buckingham Road neighbour. Fashions for males were changing fast along with everyday events in the local community. I had already left in search of a Fast Life in London and things were definitely not as they used to be! A six-foot conger eel had been found at Northfleet Power Station, then in the process of being rebuilt, and there was even talk of St

Botolph's vicarage being demolished. Members of the local Youth For Nuclear Disarmament were about to maintain a twenty-four-hour vigil at the Clock Tower in Gravesend in honour of the dead of Hiroshima and local teenagers were told the group was an Inspiration but Bernard was in no mood to join them. More pertinent to him was the fact that Colyer Road School was about to trial a period of Mufti and there had been a great deal of discussion between boys and staff as to what constituted Suitable School Clothing. Smart Casual appeared to be the order of the day and during his wanderings past the men's outfitters in both Perry Street and Gravesend he had totally acquainted himself with what that particular Look demanded. The only problem was how to secure it, particularly as his available funds did not even stretch to a trim never mind a re-style at Wandings the Barbers or even an after-school helping of chips from Lads' Fish & Chips shop nearby.

Relating the tale he no longer remembered which of the Waterdales cousins had passed on to him the Silver Lurex jacket but he vividly recalled that it closely resembled a much coveted item displayed in the window of a store in Gravesend High Street. His heart missed a number of beats in his delirium of joy when it was bestowed upon him and it mattered little that the garment was several sizes too big. Old Nan told him in no uncertain terms that he looked like Some Pearly Bleeding King in it and even our mother regarded it with more than a modicum of doubt. However, knowing how unlikely it would have been for her to ever countenance such a purchase, even in the improbable event of him ever managing to attain the required six pounds seven shillings and sixpence of likely cost, her reservations were completely ignored. In fact so impatient was he to show it off he could not be dissuaded from giving it its first outing by wearing it to school the very next day.

Bernard was totally confident that the jacket in all its Lurex glory was fundamentally so stylish that all his school mates and probably a sizeable chunk of the staff as well, would be green with envy. For once in his life he, Bernard John Hendy of 28 York Road, Northfleet would be seen as a trend-setter in the area of male fashion. He blissfully contemplated the possible secondary effects of the newly elevated position among his peers the Jacket would undoubtedly ensure. An invitation to join the In-Crowd for Saturday night dancing sessions at the Co-op in Harmer Street? Very likely! He would, of course, first have to learn a few dance steps but clad in Silver Lurex that should not be beyond him. Even his ability to absorb subjects like Mathematics might now be possible earning him sudden and unexpected respect from the Maths teacher … 'Applying yourself at last Hendy. I always knew you had it in you….' A pleasing possibility.

The fact that the first wearing coincided with the Headmaster's Monday Morning Assembly rhetoric on Casual Clothing Suitable for the Classroom he felt was fortunate – indeed fortuitous. He was still beaming with shimmering pride and superiority when he was called onto the rostrum as a demonstration of what must surely be Outstanding Schoolboy Sophistication. He obligingly turned a full circle and slightly lifted his arms in order that the full Glory of the Glossy Garment should be revealed. It was some minutes before he realised that he was being held to ridicule and that he might possibly be alone in believing that Silver Lurex trimmed with velvet came anywhere close to good taste even within the Colyer Road Schoolboy Fraternity of 1961.

My brother was an exceptional raconteur and all of us that evening sitting at the dinner table at Cape Wrath Lodge laughed heartily when he recounted this probably only slightly embellished story of youthful folly. Even so, it was all too evident that regardless of the material success that had befallen him in the intervening years and the impressive row of jackets for every occasion that now hung in his first floor wardrobe, at the age of sixty-seven he was still more than a little disconcerted in the telling of it.

# The Vacuum Cleaner

Those who were in their early teens when they emerged from the oppression of 1950s-style dire poverty could develop particularly idiosyncratic behaviour patterns. From within the winter warmth and security of his home in Scotland, and after the dozen or so guests attending the 2009 Family Gathering had retired to bed, Bernard sipped on his late night Lagavulin and told me of his own decidedly odd reaction to a vacuum cleaner.

Until the particular purchase was made the intricacies of housework at 28 York Road had been carried out with the aid of a broom and dustpan and brush just as it had for years. It was true that the privileged few of our neighbours, those owning large Axminster style rugs that they determinedly called Carpets, also owned strange objects of bat-like shape called Carpet Beaters. Very occasionally, because the lifting was more than difficult to manage, these Carpets were manhandled onto washing lines and mercilessly beaten. On occasions I watched in fascination and wished we owned such a floor covering that might be publicly and ostentatiously thrashed, not realising that soon Carpet Beating would become a thing of the past. We were in no danger of ever owning a carpet and our own rugs were firmly called Mats and mostly home made on winter evenings. Nonetheless they were still fiercely protected by our mother who was still disinclined to allow visitors to step on them too thoughtlessly and was to remain so.

It was not even certain that the services of vacuum cleaners were actually needed in the little Victorian terrace cottages when a soft broom from Rayners' the hardware shop in Northfleet High Street had always done a reasonable job. By the time our family had taken the plunge and become owners of one, however, our mother was remarking that a Hoover would certainly Break the Back of what housework needed to be done and make cleaning under the beds a Snip and a Doddle. She pointed out, unnecessarily, that everyone else in the street now owned these labour-saving machines and kept them in their converted coal cupboards so it was Not Before Time. Our coal cupboard was not as yet converted because we still went in for coal fires but the Hoover could definitely be kept upstairs in the corner beside her wardrobe.

So long after they made their way into adjacent homes, the purchase was finally made from The Rainbow Stores in Gravesend on Tick, putting down a pound and paying off the remainder at five shillings weekly for months to come. I had long since left for my life in London by this time and Bernard would have been about fourteen or fifteen and very nearly ready to join the workforce. Although housework was not generally something that had ever greatly appealed to him, he was for some reason positively dazzled and overwhelmed by what he now maintained was an Electrolux but agreed might equally well may have been a Hoover 800 or even a Constellation. He was stunned by its crisp, clean lines, hypnotized by the glitter of the steel piping and the way the hose curled at his feet as he breathlessly elected to be the one to unpack it. So awe inspiring was this piece of home technology to an adolescent decidedly out of kilter with the reality of modern life, that he became convinced the entire neighbourhood would be similarly impressed with this particularly upmarket Hendy Household purchase. This was because though they may have been vacuum cleaner owners themselves for a year or two, not a single one of them could possibly own a machine quite as dazzling in its complexity and beauty.

For the next ten days, instead of going to school he waited impatiently in the York Road Alley for my mother to leave for her Dinner Lady's job at Gravesend Girls' Grammar School before quietly letting himself back into the house. Once inside he reverently lifted the magnificent machine from its place beside the wardrobe and gazed upon it in hypnotized silence. Then he slung it respectfully across his shoulders and set out on a circuit of the neighbourhood so that all might witness its glory. Up York Road he strode, along Shepherd Street, then turning right into Buckingham Road leisurely strolling past The Volley, the popular local public house before finally returning via the backyard of Number 28 where the magnificence of the machine was once again hidden from view and safely restored into its cardboard casing.

Long afterwards, in 2015, he recalled with clarity the enormous sense of fulfilment he got from this ritual and was convinced he grew at least two inches taller during that time. All and sundry were now aware that he, Bernard John Hendy, came from a home where luxury items such as that he paraded upon his shoulders, were not just a dream, but a reality!

# A Constant Approach To Matrimony

The Constant cousins all seemed to be getting married from 1953 onwards and on one occasion my services were even required as a bridesmaid which should have been exciting and perhaps would have been a few years previously when playing Weddings was a popular game among the under-twelves of York Road, Buckingham Road and Tooley Street. In those days the most testing aspect of that particular game was persuading a Real Live Boy to play and although I could have forced my brother into the game he was too young for it to be much fun. Colin Bardoe could always be relied upon but was always demanding about what the bride wore and how she should conduct herself and his twin, Alan, was never all that keen in the first place. I remember we were all most impressed when Kathleen McCarthy whose parents ran The Queen's Head on the Hill and were thought to be well-off, was bridesmaid at a family wedding and had her hair permed for the occasion. She consented to answer a lot of questions and told us that the dress she was to wear was pale blue velvet with a sweetheart neckline.

When my older cousin Margaret got married to Young Jock who was very handsome and drove a red sports car, the dress I was to wear was disappointing to say the least. A cast-off from yet another wedding from her father's side of the family, slightly grubby aquamarine imitation satin and rather too small for me. Aunt Mag said I was piling on the pounds but we all knew that as a fourteen-year-old I shouldn't be trying to force myself into a dress more suitable for someone of eleven. Margaret wondered if we could let it out and my mother said she would try which horrified me. As I have said before, she was enthusiastic but had little talent for dressmaking.

The wedding was fairly uneventful except that I managed to get very drunk on gin and had to be almost carried back to the house in Iron Mill Lane and put to bed with instant coffee. A year or so later the happy couple decided they were not meant for each other after all and parted in what seemed to be an amicable fashion. This Simply Wasn't Done in the mid-fifties, particularly in Roman Catholic families, and so of course not only did the neighbours gossip but the immediate family gossiped even more in hushed and horrified whispers. Because ours was a family where intimate matters were not openly discussed at all, lies and fabrications became thus piled onto secrets. I was more recently surprised to find that in certain corners of the family this is still happening today despite the fact that we now live within a far less surreptitious, cloak and dagger environment. My mother and Old Nan both blamed the man Margaret worked for, known simply as The Boss at that time, because at Easter and Whitsun he whisked her off to Paris to help him take care of urgent jobs that simply couldn't wait until after the Bank Holiday. Old Nan said everybody knew exactly what kind of jobs they would be and not only my mother agreed, but several other aunts also. Those who knew more of the sordid details added that it was his poor wife they felt sorry for. Margaret's own mother, Aunt Mag, was tight lipped and held her head firmly in the air humming *We'll Gather Lilacs*.

My cousin Pat was married in a great hurry at about the same time though she was only just sixteen and we all pretended not to know that she was, as Old Nan put it, In The Pudding Club. One of my older male cousins described this as Being Up The Duff which none of us really understood at that time but then he was in the Merchant Navy and came out with a lot of odd statements. The only bridesmaid Pat had was Little Violet who did not get a great many treats and was highly excited in a pink crochet dress generously made by one of the aunts. Less than two months later Pat gave birth to baby Sharon causing all female family members to forget their previous censure and disapproval and vie with each other for turns holding the newborn. Pat, despite all predictions of doom and gloom for her possible future, remained married and had several more children.

When Cousin June walked up the aisle a great deal was expected of the arrangements for the Do afterwards because she was known to be a bit of a Show Off. June had issued various appeals on the invitations to the guests concerning such matters as not wearing what she described as Dangly Ear Rings or colours that were too bright. My mother said that if any more demands were made then she wouldn't go at all but we all knew she didn't mean it. June's wedding differed from those we were accustomed to in that there was no Sit Down Wedding Breakfast but everyone stood up and ate a great many cocktail sausages and bits of cheese on sticks instead, and had only beer and wine to drink. A live band played subdued music and nobody was allowed to dance the Conger Eel. Many of the guests were disappointed but shortly after the event the newly-weds disappeared to South Africa and were not seen again for many years. Aunt Maud then read excerpts to us from June's letters home, especially bits that said she had a Girl coming in each week to do the ironing and the heavy work. The aunts whispered among themselves that it was a Black Girl that was being referred to because Over There the Whites were not allowed to do any real work. Old Nan said she'd be buggered if she'd want one anyway and as for herself she had always been capable of doing her own ironing. Everyone knew that she didn't know one end of a modern electric iron from the other but of course nobody said that within her hearing.

    When mutterings were made about whether I would be Next I said nothing having very recently discarded my first boyfriend Barrie of the Flint House in Springhead Road. Aunt Mag observed in rather acerbic tones that I would have to get myself a Young Man first and one of the others tut tutted that I was No Longer Courting. My mother said not for the first time that it was unlikely I would do any better than Him Who I Dumped and I was a fool but then I always had been apparently. Later when the visiting relatives had gone back to Crayford she remarked in a clearly aggravated tone that she could have done without Mag's opinions considering what became of the marriage of her Margaret and Jock who very soon was known as That Poor Sod Jock. It rapidly became clear over the next few weeks that Margaret was now living at The Boss's new flat in Old Bexley and that his wife and children had refused to leave the marital home. Aunt Martha said you could hardly blame them and still referred to him as The Boss even though he had now become Ron to most of us. This state of affairs caused even greater consternation within the family because despite their more than humble origins they were generally unified in turning a staunchly upright and moral front to the world in general. To her credit, with the ongoing support of her steadfastly loyal parents, Margaret ignored the wagging tongues and continued to regularly pay visits to the family even when she seemed to be strangely gaining a great deal of weight and had swapped dirndl skirts and high heels for stretchy Swiss knit suits and sensible flat shoes. Nobody openly discussed her Condition and once Baby Nigel appeared on the scene he was welcomed by one and all.

Around this time the old Vicarage by St Botolph's Church on The Hill was demolished and a number of smart and modern houses built in its place; the little enclave was called Vicarage Drive. My mother had observed the annihilation of the Vicarage with some regret but when Margaret burst through the front door of 28 York Road one afternoon to say that she and Ron had just bought one of the Vicarage Drive homes there was rejoicing over the teacups and I was informed of this exciting development with all due haste. When I innocently enquired if that meant they were now actually married my mother reverted back several years and said Layos For Meddlers which I thought yet another inappropriate response considering I was now grown up. Whether or when they finally entered the state of matrimony is still unknown because it is not something anyone ever spoke of, particularly when Ron proceeded to shed his original persona as a Bit Of A Wide Boy and become a successful businessman. He and Margaret certainly stayed together for a long time and had three children and each was greatly loved by my mother who embarked upon the family babysitting with her usual enthusiasm and without undue comment.

For a long time I occupied the place of Chief Family Wrongdoer which began with the unwise dumping Boyfriend Barrie and his non-replacement, and then giving birth to my oldest son out of wedlock. Once in that position it is quite difficult to climb out of it as anyone who has experienced it will tell you.

# The Blissful Burgeoning of Bathrooms

Old Mr Bassent from next door maintained that the houses in York Road and the surrounding streets were more than a hundred and ten years old and would have long been Condemned if it hadn't been for The War. I was first aware of this as early as 1943 when I had no idea what being Condemned meant so later on I asked and someone said it meant they should have been pulled down long ago. This was a scary thought at the time because as a pre-schooler I was very satisfied with number twenty eight where the only available water was from the single scullery tap and definitely cold, and where what Old Nan called The Privy or The Khazi and we called The Lav was outside in what she called The Yard and we called The Garden. In order to become dissatisfied I had to get just a little bit older and more aware of the up-to-date bathroom facilities in the council houses my cousins lived in up in Crayford.

As far as our grandmother was concerned our York Road house with its very reasonable rent of seven shillings a week was a step up from her own childhood home in the crowded Closed Court off Cambridge Road Bethnal Green with shared pump and privy in the tiny inner yard and where the only access was by means of a narrow tunnel less than three feet wide. It was more than evident that general hygiene was an even greater challenge back then than for us in the more innovative 1940s with our very own galvanised bath hanging on the wall and a reliable supply of fresh, cold water in our scullery. According to Old Nan these were steps forward simply undreamed of back in the late nineteenth century when if you wanted to get yourself clean for a special occasion such as your own wedding for instance, it meant a trip to the Bath House which cost money and not to get her started on that subject.

Despite the giant steps forward however, maintaining standards of personal cleanliness was not straightforward by any means. Saturday night was always bath night and it was then our copper would be filled and a fire lit under it so that enough water could be boiled for the occasion, supplemented by pots and kettles on the stove. Naturally enough everyone bathed in the same water, starting with the children in most families which meant that the experience was both grimy and decidedly cool as the evening wore on and the adults were able to have their turn. As children our hair was washed whilst we were in the bath but I have a feeling that my mother washed hers in the stone scullery sink with jugs of warm water and always with the aid of Amami Shampoo for Fair Hair. As we all had dark hair her choice of shampoo was puzzling. Yellow Sunlight soap was used in the bath as in our house it was deemed most extravagant to bathe with the aid of any toilet soap let alone something as expensive as Pears so I could never boast of Preparing to Be a Beautiful Lady.

Keeping clean was time consuming and between baths I don't remember anything other than brief face and hands washing known as a Lick and a Promise although my mother definitely admired those who went in for more regular cleanliness rituals. She frequently commented on the practice of one neighbour, who she knew for a fact had a lovely wash every day and never missed come rain or shine. This daily wash was carried out after dinner in the early afternoon and you could apparently see she had washed her neck without fail each time and what's more she was also in the habit of putting on lovely clean blouses, a fresh one every day, never mind all that ironing.

By the time I was seven or eight years old and reading a great many Enid Blyton books I was, as previously stated more than once, definitely more than keen on the idea of proper bathrooms and indoor lavatories. Just imagine being able to run a warm bath whenever you fancied it. Or the bliss of being able to use the toilet without putting on raincoat and wellington boots if it was raining. And these aspirations were not entirely due to Enid Blyton because as I have already mentioned there were the cousins, all of whom now seeming to have found themselves living in houses that boasted the most desirable facilities. Even my mother whose bathroom ambitions were not nearly as pronounced as my own and nowhere near as ambitious as my brother's, was heard to make certain comments. Her sister Mag, she said, could be a Dirty Cow at times and you only had to look at the state of that lovely new inside lavatory all stained for want of a bit of bleach. I stored the bleach information for future use and vowed that I would never be such a Dirty Cow as my aunt.

My brother was to become even more preoccupied with the delights of indoor plumbing but considerable time was to pass before I quite understood the strength of his passion. As he moved towards the lofty world of the property owner Bernard began to show a greater and greater interest in sanitary arrangements, his favourite room of any house he was to live in at any future stage clearly being the bathroom. As time progressed his bathrooms grew both in number and in extravagance sporting tiling techniques that the fussiest of Romans would have been envious of and shower arrangements so complex that the uninitiated hesitated before entering them. He firmly maintained that this hunger for all matters sanitary had come about because of his conviction that as a child he smelled bad enough for others to avoid him. Other children, he said, called him Stink Bum. This may or may not have been entirely true because as he grew up Bernard also grew ever more flexible with truth.

If it was true it had probably originated because of his persistent bed-wetting which although not all that unusual in boys, went on far longer than anyone expected it to. Bernard was still wetting the bed as he approached his sixteenth birthday and the bedsheets were hung out of the upper back window on a daily basis obvious to all and causing him a great deal of embarrassment. The side effects of this unfortunate habit of enuresis were rather more than a weekly bath in the scullery could hope to contain. Our mother was concerned enough by the time he was fourteen to attempt to persuade him to avoid all liquids after midday and on one occasion brought the subject up with Dr Outred who was not able to offer a great deal of hope. Old Nan on the other hand as usual had a positive suggestion which rather surprisingly involved matrimony. Getting Him Married, she maintained, would put a stop to all that Pissing the Bed Malarkey before you could say Bob's

Your Uncle or Fanny's Your Aunt. I couldn't help wondering what would happen if he urinated over his new wife but could not think of a delicate way of putting the possibility so I remained silent.

He was of course very much married very early on in life and I was never quite game enough to make further enquiry regarding the bed wetting. On the other hand the proliferation of elaborate and ostentatious bathrooms that played such a dominant role in his life were clearly an indication of something unusually significant.

## The Houses of Robinia Avenue

In the 1940s and 1950s we lesser mortals of York Road, Tooley Street, Buckingham Road and Shepherd Street considered the three Avenues and one Grove that lay on the far side of Dover Road to be quite exclusive and the dwellings therein almost impossibly desirable. Those fortunate families giving Lime, Robinia or Plane Avenues, or Laburnum Grove as their home address were extended a certain amount of deference from the butcher, chemist and greengrocer – esteem that the rest of us were definitely unlikely ever to be the recipients of. Bernard held Robinia Avenue in particular in very high regard as did our mother for I know for a fact that I was pushed up and down that hallowed Avenue as a baby in my high pram simply for the entertainment value.

The high pram itself was something of a luxury and years later I was told it was bought On Tick from Arthur Barnes' Rainbow Stores because not only did he go in for fair prices and a wide stock range but his after sales service was apparently second to none. Hire Purchase was in its infancy at The Rainbow and did not take off in its later more recognisable form until after the war, but certainly late in 1939 you could organise what was sometimes called A Laying By with certain stores and pay five shillings a week and once your chosen item had reached the halfway point towards complete payment you could take it home with you. It was because of some similar arrangement that I ended up with a rather more stylish pram than might otherwise have been my fate and hence, perhaps, the regular outings to the various Groves and Avenues that befitted such a baby carriage.

As stated our mother was as admiring of Robinia Avenue as in later years her son was to be. It was a residential road where smart interwar residences stood side by side each proudly displaying its small front garden and just beyond, a door to the vestibule where raincoats and muddy Wellington boots could be left and the dog's lead or harness could be stored if you actually owned a dog. But then the people of Robinia Avenue did seem to keep dogs and were particularly fond of Cocker Spaniels and Corgis. Pausing deferentially outside one of the wrought iron gates, I was told before I was one year old that instead of kitchens some of these homes had Kitchenettes that were a mere passageway fitted with cooker, worktop and sink, galley style; what progress! Some of the houses featured stained and coloured glass in the form of decorative leadlights, adding enormously to their overall appeal. Tiling was also greatly admired and being impervious to frost tiles were used outdoors for forecourts and doorsteps and could also be seen via tantalising glimpses, sometimes even on the walls of the porches. Our wartime neighbour Old Mrs Bassent said that the New Estates in a place called Welwyn Garden City were all like Laburnum Grove and The Avenues and that one day we might perhaps take a day trip together to see this phenomenon for ourselves.

I seemed destined to be pushed in the high pram for much longer than was usual and I must have been nearly two years old when I was told one morning shortly after a particularly active overnight period of incendiary bombing that we were in for a Real Treat because it was a day when we might actually see inside the vestibule of one of the Robinia Avenue homes! My high pram was to be exchanged for a pushchair courtesy of an advertisement in the window of Ripleys the Greengrocers. I clearly recall my hair being neatly brushed for the occasion and tied with new hair ribbons, and being put into white socks and my best shiny black shoes that were just a little too tight and made me protest volubly when required to walk in them. I have a vivid memory of the journey back when the green lollipop I had been given to stop me screaming both for the return of my high pram and the agony of the tight shoe problem, got stuck in the wheels of the alien pushchair, new, modern, green and already much hated. Sadly I remember nothing of the house with the vestibule and whether or not we might have also got to see the narrow kitchenette but my mother waxed lyrical about the baby vehicle switch for months so it was certainly a very rewarding exchange of goods as far as she was concerned.

The general attraction of the desirable residences did not entirely diminish as I grew older, and from time to time Molly from No 31 and I would choose the Avenues for our occasional contemplative walks, during which we planned our futures including husbands, homes, careers and in my case even the names of my possible children and what they might wear on a daily basis. I remember planning pink tweed coats with matching skirts for my two imaginary daughters and even hesitated for a moment before abandoning a similar outfit for their younger brother.

It was years before I realised that the much sought-after area just around the corner from Dover Road had also had a significant effect upon my younger brother and most particularly so where his relationship with his future Father in Law was concerned. Bernard told me that he had immediately become inordinately fond of Reg, his new fiancée's father, and despite Bernard's many failings it seems evident that the feeling was mutual. Reg certainly went out of his way to be more than fatherly and helpful towards the teenager who was to become the father of his first grandchild. Considering the extreme youth of the young couple and my brother's lack of Old Fashioned Prospects, this attitude of paternalistic concern and affection is rather surprising. Any initial surprise concerning the relationship between Reg and his son-in-law-to-be could only turn to wonder and astonishment when the actual breadth of my brother's deception and duplicity was finally untangled and revealed.

My sister-in-law herself said that she became aware quite early on in their relationship that the young man she loved was not always totally honest with her. Pragmatism prevented her from delving too deeply into his various webs of fantasy, however. She did not believe for a moment that my poor mother, still living in York Road, Northfleet, and quite obviously in financial need, drove a Citroen which she parked in Dover Road. Neither did she believe that this Citroen enthusiast owned several properties in Spain. These claims seemed unlikely to Janice. And she thought it dubious that Nellie was Bernard's long lost and only recently rediscovered Real Mother and that he had been adopted as a small child into a more affluent Robinia Avenue family. Furthermore it seemed doubtful that he was nearly twenty-one years old when other local lads who claimed to have been in his class at school were only just reaching their eighteenth birthdays. His declaration that he was a pop singer with a well-known band also seemed improbable.

Janice was an undeniably astute and perceptive young woman but her all-too-trusting father, despite his years of undoubted success in the business of supplying paint and wallpaper to the citizens of both Islington and the Medway Towns, clearly was not. It later became evident that Reg had touching faith in the various fanciful tales told to him by his youthful son-in-law. Not only did he appear to uncritically accept the Pop Band story which explained Bernard's lack of more mundane Work History, he did not for one moment query his age and even contacted me at the approach of an entirely imaginary twenty-first birthday to ask if it would be in order for him to Put On A Bit Of A Do to celebrate the event. It's very hard to know what to say under such circumstances and I think I said very little, hoping that the crisis would pass because by this time the young couple were already married and living quite happily above the shop in Camden Passage, at The Angel where my brother was now the manager. Whatever conversation passed between us, Reg did indeed Put On A Bit Of A Do and a hall was hired, we all dressed up for the occasion, bottles of something very like champagne were served along with smoked salmon savouries and Bernard celebrated his twenty-first birthday at a time when he was only eighteen and a half years old, and our mother even tut-tutted that I had not brought with me a suitable gift.

There was undoubtedly, despite everything, a bond of love and respect between Bernard and his father-in-law and over time, with a fair amount of fast talking, the complications in their early relationship emanating from the tidal wave of fantasy my brother created around himself, were resolved. Years later Bernard confided that the very worst teething problem of the relationship had been extricating himself from Robinia Avenue and the fiction that he lived there in a more than noticeably smart corner house complete with stained glass, tiles and a fortunately friendly Corgi.

During the months leading up to their wedding, he visited Janice and her family at Istead Rise several evenings each week and ever-helpful Reg had become in the habit of dropping him home; but not to York Road where he was to later still maintain his Recently Rediscovered Citroen-driving Real mother lived in poverty. Heart in mouth he regularly and with an astonishing degree of confidence, entered the front gate of the house in Robinia Avenue where invariably the corgi gave a welcoming bark, calling out a jovial 'Thanks & Cheerio' to Reg before stooping to greet the animal then secreting himself behind the hedge until the car had turned back towards Istead Rise. Then, whistling with relief, he sauntered home to York Road leaving an ever-confused and wistfully whining canine behind him!

In more ways than one and over a very long period of time, as a family we were individually much involved with the Desirable Dwellings of Robinia Avenue.

# The Robin Hood of Wrotham Hill

As previously pointed out, our grandmother was not averse to general pilfering of one kind and another and it's more than likely that this habit had its roots in the extreme poverty of her earliest years. I can't ever remember her coming to the attention of the police on account of it which could have been due to uncommon good luck or more probably to the customary code of silence that was inclined to govern such behaviour and its consequences in families like ours. She definitely had what were called Run Ins with authority on other matters such as drunkenness and unruly behaviour but her frequent thefts from other people's washing lines seemed to be at all times overlooked. This would have been considered a good thing because within our family ranks as long as stealing did not involve getting caught then it appeared to be largely condoned and often even the trigger for minor celebration. As we were at the same time firmly adhered to the doctrines of the Catholic Church it took me a long time to work my way through this particular dichotomy; it seemed confusing and to some extent still does.

The case of our 'Aunt Freda who was not to be addressed as Aunt', was less bewildering because this particular Crayford Constant was well known as a habitual thief and con woman but because of her special position as The Baby of the Constant Family, and the fact that she was thought not to have complete control over her various urges, her misdeeds had always been tolerated by parents, siblings and also the local priest.

Our mother, the second-born in the family, had early memories more concerned with drunkenness and hunger than whether any food or clothing that made its way to the Constants had been paid for or simply purloined from retailers' shelves or filched from neighbours. Even so, years later she vehemently objected to her youngest sister's persistent deceptions. She said that Freda would have the Shirt Off Your Back if you didn't keep your wits about you and you needed Eyes In The Back Of Your Head when she was around. Old Nan was invariably quick to leap to the defence of her youngest child and explain to anyone inclined to listen that there was No Harm In Her, a view not universally shared. My brother and I were quick to notice that our mother's own petty thieving increased with the death of our father though for many years involved such insignificant items such as cans of baked beans and the occasional packet of Garibaldi biscuits and mostly we chose to ignore it or as she would have said herself, Turned A Blind Eye. It was not a topic we were comfortable bringing up and we were both quite grown up before we actually openly discussed these episodes of lawbreaking together and even then it was obvious we still felt somewhat awkward and disloyal about the dialogue.

Bernard's first wife, Janice, having been raised within a far more straightforward and honest environment, had considerably less reluctance for the debate and said that although she had found it very odd that every time a cupboard was opened in my mother's cramped kitchen a dozen cans of baked beans were likely to topple out, she regarded her not merely as a thief but rather as a kind of latter day Robin Hood. Janice insisted that there was more than just a minor element of the redistribution of riches in my mother's behaviour. Urged to further clarify she explained that she had found her mother-in-law particularly practiced at reallocating expensive items of children's clothing around to those she decided were in most need and that her own small son, Merlin, had been the fortunate recipient of a number of such items during the first year of his life. Naturally enough, now she had given voice to the aberrant behaviour, even though my brother cowered back into his chair looking vaguely embarrassed, I demanded to be told the full story.

Janice said that the situation under review largely concerned my older cousin Margaret, she who had been Carrying On with Ron, her new boss once she left the job in the shoe shop in Dartford. By the time Janice and Bernard had met, Margaret had not only discarded Jock her first husband, but The Boss had left his own wife and family, and they had both left the rumour and tittle tattle of Crayford behind them and set up home properly in Vicarage Drive Northfleet where the neighbours knew nothing of the scandal associated with them. Later on even Old Nan, not given to compliments, had said that considering what could have happened and often did with girls like Margaret, she had Done Well in the end. As to the snags concerning The Boss's reluctance to extricate himself from his Roman Catholic marriage, this was not openly discussed by any of us and Nellie pursed her lips and shook her head disapprovingly at me when I was once foolish enough to bring it up, talking of Layos

For Meddlers in quite a threatening manner so I knew better than to persist. Whether or not Margaret was to be made an Honest Woman of became irrelevant with the advent of the 1960s and the birth of her three children. Eventually the house in Vicarage Drive was disposed of and an even more impressive residence in the form of old farm house was acquired at Wrotham Hill together with a number of farm cottages. My brother was foolishly confident that he might persuade Ron the Boss to part with one of the near derelict cottages at a reasonable price since it was his own dream to live in a truly rural environment where the study of bird life would be placed conveniently close by. However, that dream was firmly dispatched into the ether and was to take decades to finally achieve when Ron decided he would rather demolish all the old farm buildings. This action caused a great deal of negative comment among the relatives and even Old Nan, not always a total supporter of my brother or myself or in fact any of her many grandchildren, was heard to say that even a fool could see that the cottages were habitable and Ron suddenly descended from being halfway acceptable to becoming for a while As Ignorant As Pigshit. Perhaps it was simply that Ron did not want Bernard as a near neighbour which was understandable as he already had my mother as a semi-permanent child-minding house guest and he might have feared a full on invasion of the immediate family with me bringing up the rear together with my infant son. However, for many years the cottage demolition was to greatly irk poor Bernard who saw it as needless vandalism and this view was generally supported by my mother though she was considerably more reluctant to voice her opinion.

Baby Nigel, Margaret's first born, was a much doted upon infant which is probably not unusual with first children and from time to time his parents would bring back expensive hand-embroidered silk baby outfits from Paris and Lucerne on their Urgent Trips Abroad that so frequently coincided with Bank Holiday weekends. But with such an eager child minder as Nellie, ever-admiring of Nigel and his lavish wardrobe, who can blame them for the timing of their Mini Breaks?

Janice and Bernard's own baby was not born until Christmas Eve 1965 on the very evening that our grandmother died after staggering back from The Jolly Farmers with what was to be the final half bottle of gin of her life. Little Nigel had already been joined by a younger sister and brother, Jayne and Peter. All three of Margaret's children would almost certainly have outgrown the distinctive hand-embroidered silk garments from Continental Europe and these no doubt had been folded away awaiting the birth of some possible future baby. Things would not quite go to plan, however, because at some stage during her frequent child minding stays at the house at Wrotham Hill, my mother had decided to distribute the baby finery more equitably around the pool of family infants and my sister-in-law found herself the recipient of a most impressive summer outfit for her young son, then several months old. She was astonished she said, for several reasons, the first being that when she commented upon the hand stitching and the French label inside the tiny collar my mother had insisted she had Picked Up the ensemble for Next to

Nothing at Gravesend Market from Old Strongy the well-known Gravesend Market Trader. Sid Strong had worked the market every Saturday for thirty years, moving on to Petticoat Lane on Sunday mornings and over time although he vended canteen after canteen of cutlery and a never-ending line in Dinner Services, not to mention thousands of china ornaments and electric toasters, none of us could remember him ever dealing in upmarket baby clothes. The declared origins of the gift therefore seemed highly improbable. Furthermore, Janice's baby was accustomed to wearing ordinary Stretch & Gros and she wondered whether there would ever be an occasion grand enough on which he could don the dazzling outfit for an hour or two. However, her parents' wedding anniversary party in Chatham a few weeks later seemed to provide the perfect opportunity. Janice said Baby Merlin looked quite splendid in the finery so much so that Bernard took a number of photographs of him. They set off from Islington bound for Chatham that Sunday afternoon in high spirits.

It was Bernard who suggested that on the way they might drop into the house on Wrotham Hill and say hello to his cousin and Ron who had by this time all but stopped being referred to as Margaret's Fancy Man or The Boss by the various Aunts and was almost one hundred per cent accepted. When the young family arrived, my mother was pouring tea on the terrace at the back of the house, completely and happily involved in the role she had adopted of being a kind of Faithful Family Retainer. Everyone seemed delighted to see the unexpected visitors and they were ushered into seats and urged to drink tea. Janice was halfway through her first cup when she noticed that Margaret who was sitting opposite her seemed to be transfixed by baby Merlin on his father's knee beaming in his dazzling infant apparel. Well why not? He was a simply gorgeous baby after all. A further moment passed before she realised that it was the hand-embroidered silk baby clothes that Margaret seemed so taken with. Janice had already begun on the explanation for the finery, purchased by his doting Grandma at Gravesend Market for Next to Nothing from Old Strongy when realisation dawned and she knew by Margaret's astonished expression and her faint echoing of 'Old Strongy?' that nothing was more certain than that a Robin Hood episode had taken place. In the same moment she knew that there was little further that could be said or done by way of explanation that would save the day. The best and only action she decided was to refuse a second cup of tea and hurry onwards towards the wedding anniversary celebrations in Chatham. The unplanned visit of the Hendy Family had lasted a mere twenty minutes.

It was a long time before they returned to the Farmhouse on Wrotham Hill, and neither was any invitation extended to them to do so. Strangely, my mother's relationship with her niece and family seemed only to strengthen but possibly that was in large part due to the fact that willing child minders were hard to find in that particular corner of Kent and possibly also my mother's undoubted improbable explanation of the incident that Margaret persuaded herself to accept. Whatever the actual truth of the matter was, when the Robin Hood story was told to me thirty years after the event I listened with more than a little interest and began to rethink the origins of unexpected luxury items I had occasionally found myself in possession of as a teenager. For instance the No Longer Required though clearly nearly new woollen dressing gown I had inherited from The Lovells when my mother first worked for them. It was the very first dressing gown of my life because at that time they seemed to be garments belonging to people in books, not those from working class families like me. Even at the time I was struck by the bountiful munificence of the gift. Now I wondered what had happened to the note of thanks I had written for my mother to deliver on her next working day.

# Family Facts & Fantasies

When I recently in a general fashion posed the question as to the wisdom of writing about Predators from the Past, those family members whose behaviour towards young female relatives should have been curbed, the reactions were immediate, diverse, thought-provoking. Overall the feeling was that it is better by far to stay silent. Do not awaken sleeping dogs. Roman Catholic Families still reflect the attitudes of their Church and prefer to continue to offer robust protection to miscreants where certain matters of offending are concerned. And although not entirely surprising, in this day and age it is more than a little disappointing. But is it in the great scheme of things any more disheartening than the veil of secrecy that is traditionally drawn over a whole raft of other, infinitely less contentious Family Matters many would prefer to dismiss permanently into the nether regions of the Undiscussable? It would be reassuring to be able to say that such attitudes are behind the times, outdated, even archaic and in these more enlightened times we of the twenty-first century being so utterly up to date in outlook find them laughingly old-fashioned. Except that so many of us don't. Our grandmother and aunts were highly shamed by the presence of Queenie the Hermaphrodite in their ranks. She was only to be spoken of in whispers and with derision. Similarly in the late 1940s our mother was deeply mortified to concede that our father was a serial adulterer and could only bring herself to openly acknowledge the fact when he had been dead for over thirty years. I am still unsure as to whether the topic was ever discussed in any depth with my brother. He seemed uncomfortable with the subject so it probably wasn't.

From the depths of her worry and concern our mother had sadly always overlooked our father's good points. An adulterer he certainly was but he was also a man with a wide range of interests and many loyal friends. He read widely, learned arias from Italian opera simply for fun and wrote poetry, each somewhat unusual interests for a working class man and maybe worthy of discussion. But he was as far as she was concerned simply designated a sexual philanderer and as she was never prepared to openly recognise the infidelity fully, his memory, together with all that was worthy about him, was forever consigned to a dark corner and he was rarely, if ever, spoken of. His son, longing for a discussion about him, always lamenting the fact that he had only limited memories of him, had only tiny tantalising glimpses of a man whose absence he mourned.

Later it was perhaps more understandable that our mother had an eagerness for my brother's growing career in crime to be overlooked. He was never going to pose a threat to the Krays or the Richardsons in the execution of his law breaking but Nellie's enthusiasm for denying that any of the increasingly alarming incidents he was involved in actually took place was disquieting. A large part of the offending was undoubtedly initially sparked from his burning desire at the age seven and eight years of age to become the owner of a pair of binoculars. This would have been a modest ambition for as keen a budding ornithologist as he was becoming at the time, if our family finances had only been just a little more healthy. Unhappily, the untimely death of our father had ensured that there was little prospect of there ever being enough disposable cash in the family for the desire to be realised and knowing that, Bernard simply tried to attain his goal by other means. The other means to him, coming from a family where casual pilfering was second nature, naturally seemed lie in his own hands. He made several early attempts at modest larceny from a second-hand shop in Gravesend but unfortunately for him the eagle eyes of the ex-Home Guard in charge of the premises defeated the plan. He abandoned that particular establishment completely when told that he was a Thieving Little Bugger and on the very next occasion he crossed the threshold the Police would be called.

Several years passed before he tackled the thorny problem of Binoculars Ownership once more. Being a little older he approached the task rather more sensibly by making sure he had the required money in his pocket before entering the camera shop on New Road where several models were enticingly displayed. In what was to become something of a habit with him he first raided our mother's modest Rainy Day Savings by determinedly searching for her new hiding place and was thus able to pay the huge sum of twelve pounds, nineteen and sixpence required. He even paved the way for ease of ownership by telling her that he was sure he had seen an abandoned pair of binoculars hanging on a tree beside The Blue Lake at Springhead, and the very next day he was going to investigate. Having carried out the bogus investigation he then wrote an invented name into the strap of the leather case – one Mr. T.E. Johnson of Swanscombe had carelessly lost his binoculars whilst bird watching. Only a couple of weeks passed before our mother, naïve though she may have been, discovering the loss of her holiday savings, began to suspect that Bernard's story might not be completely true. Whilst he was at school one day she investigated by taking T.E. Johnson's previously lost binoculars into the camera shop in New Road where she was told by the helpful owner that a young lad answering to my brother's description had bought them with cash a mere two or three weeks previously. He kindly offered to take the illicitly acquired goods back, refunding eleven pounds but retaining one pound, nineteen shillings and sixpence for the leather case. As my brother had adorned it with Mr. T.E. Johnson's details it would be impossible to sell on to another customer. Our mother was both grateful for his understanding but highly distressed by her not yet teenage son's delinquency. The Camera Shop proprietor said it was a great pity that the boy had taken to thieving but when all was said and done all he wanted was a pair of binoculars. And he had seemed such a Nice Lad too.

So unwavering was our mother's determination to utterly ignore this increasing offending, a web of deceit was hastily built around it. Later on I was never able to ascertain if anyone else in the immediate family ever became aware of it. An iron curtain of silence descended that made discussion impossible. This was unfortunate because even at the time when these things happened, though still without experience regarding emotional trauma, I was aware that the unhappy episodes had come about primarily because Bernard was missing a father's influence and it might have helped if that could have been openly debated. This was never to be the case, however, and I imagine that should I broach the subject even today I would be soundly castigated by a number of first and second cousins all keen to feel they knew my brother extremely well, especially once he had left much of the past behind and become suitably influential, yet knew him not at all.

Our father's family was no better at accepting calamitous situations and our paternal grandmother's forty-year incarceration within a mental hospital for drunkenness and picking neighbourhood fights was a luckless tale. It only worsened with embroidery and became gossip that filtered back to cause outraged astonishment to those who had been so keen on protecting her reputation from slanderous comment in the first place.

When my first son was born in the late 1960s my mother was appalled by my unmarried status and for the benefit of friends and neighbours married me off to an entirely imaginary architect. I was not able to work out whether my closest relatives were also privy to this tale because the familial rules surrounding concealment of truth dictated that the topic could never be raised. However, a few years later when I entered an Actual Marriage with a New Zealand doctor she was greatly discomfited and forced to kill off the architect and remarry me as swiftly as possible. The speed of the nuptials was purely because Medicine rated more highly than Architecture in the scale of general achievement. To this day the demise of Husband Number One is never mentioned by any of my relatives making it a difficult item for debate.

Matters concerning sexual attraction and long term attachments between men and women were customarily even more taboo and their discussion was generally prohibited at all times. Leaving a long term partner was almost unheard of because if marriages became difficult the situation was usually adjusted to. The problems of those who abandoned the marital home were largely ignored for as long as possible and finally debated only tentatively and in a kid glove atmosphere. Surprisingly, even in the more enlightened 1980s, family consternation was rife when my brother decided to walk away from his first marriage. Bernard had been a less than ideal husband and father and it seemed not altogether surprising that after twenty years he saw fit to move on from his first wife to his second. Predictably perhaps, and like his father before him, before this decision was made he had embarked with frequency upon a number of short-lived romantic relationships to the great consternation of his long-suffering spouse who continued to do her best to love and support him.

What might have been a moderately standard transition was sadly greatly complicated by the fact that two couples who had been close friends since schooldays and who had acted as Best Men and Maids of Honour at each other's weddings, now kept things simple by switching partners thus making their lives the stuff of BBC comedies. This unexpected and unlikely situation so disturbed our nearest and dearest that the many Aunts simply decided that it wasn't happening. It was just a vicious and unfounded rumour that could not possibly be spoken of even though the truth was clearly visible to most of those around us and the details of the partner switch so sensational and scandalous that it caused months of gossip in North Kent. It is perhaps effortlessly easy to comprehend the reluctance to acknowledge the rapidly unfolding drama but unhappily such attitudes only aid and abet the layers of secrets and lies that for no very good reason thrive and flourish within families where Truth has little value.

Aghast or amused bystanders are always destined to be forever confused by the end result of certain human behaviours and eventually are given to understand that just a few family members know the Whole Truth of what the reprobates are up to whilst others are aware of partial truths and a further much less informed group know little or nothing at all because for some reason they need to be Protected. And whilst Protecting the Young is completely logical, there is surely a case for querying why protection needs to continue into their adulthood. Sadly, such mind-sets become entrenched even though they serve merely to foster misgivings because in an environment of distrust it is challenging for any one of us to make sensible decisions as to what can be discussed and with whom. Possibly that was not entirely uncommon thirty years ago and we might be advised to simply analyse it alongside the underlying social bigotry that also existed at the time. But surely things have changed by now in this enlightened first quarter of the twenty first century?

Yet have they? As far as relationship break-ups are concerned, these carry with them such a raft of damaged emotions it is easy to see how it becomes simpler not to examine a subject that is agonisingly painful. This certainly appeared to be the case when my brother, true to form perhaps, decided that the time had come for him to discard Wife No 2 on account of an unwise passion for a young woman it was said he had met at a the Stag Party organised for a friend who was himself in the throes of moving on from one relationship to another. Had our mother still lived she might have secretly felt that this particular situation was bound to happen sooner or later because she knew he might well turn out to be A Chip Off the Old Block. But her concerns would not have been as great as those she had felt on the demise of his first marriage, always maintaining that Janice had been A Very Nice Girl. She'd never taken to Wife No 2 at all, heaping the entire blame for the marital discord and destruction solely upon her shoulders and describing her as An Uppity Tart.

Nevertheless Wife No 2 now underwent considerable suffering and wondered where she had gone wrong in her steering of the relationship and pondered upon the decades of wasted energy and effort. Bernard, however, remained exasperatingly upbeat and positive because in spite of the ripples of chaos he was responsible for he was In Love and that was all that really mattered to him. It's a fact that in human affiliations one person will always be destined to suffer the greater anguish when partnerships unravel. The humiliation of being seen as no longer valued when a long-term partner signals their intention to move on cannot be truly understood by those in more secure relationships and so it was for Wife No 2 who fought valiantly to save the marriage and failed miserably because her husband was more intent upon it not being salvaged. In such situations it therefore becomes ever more logical that Mythology is fostered whilst Truth withers and with time those who seek to question the Mythology are rapidly labelled Liars of the First Order.

So what of those dark predators from times past we started with? Those who heaped their inappropriate behaviours onto the young and the unprotected? Does there ever come a time when their transgressions can be exposed and the torment they inflicted be examined? Or does it do no good to Bring It All Up? To be fair the behaviour does not seem to do much long term damage. Are the victims simply making far too much Fuss About Nothing? Did they in fact Ask for It in some cases? It was all a very long time ago so should we begin to accept the parameters of Folklore rather than face what an unfortunate few once knew to be Facts? With the passage of the years it becomes ever more feasible that the transgressions of the wrongdoers are protected alongside more run of the mill misdeeds. Does it do any good to heap misery upon their descendants? The defence of Wrongdoing begins tentatively at first simply with the passing of time. Then time creeps up alongside accuracy soundlessly, surreptitiously and irrevocably stealing certainty. Its relentless passage can be traced in the shifting boundaries of honour and integrity. Time will always be the ultimate Victor.

## First and Last Loves

When my brother died so unexpectedly in an African village early in April 2016, it was only days before what would have been his sixty-ninth birthday. There followed no announcements, no funeral to mark his passing, and no published obituary detailing his life and achievements, in fact none of the fundamental trimmings we have come to expect that sit alongside any departure from life. The customary ritual of a funeral service, the publication in newspapers of the time and place, the notices then issued by others who are unable to attend but wish their salute to the departed to be noted, the flowers, and the words spoken are all for those left behind. The Wake that usually accompanies the burial allows friends and family to share memories of the deceased and is not simply a time for lamentation but also for reflection and laughter. For Bernard there were none of these essential rites of passage and so his essence remained suspended and had he been able to do so he would undoubtedly have noted himself that it was beginning to look as if he had never really existed in the first place. And those who could remember that far back might have even noticed that in death as in life he deftly mirrored aspects of our father. Perhaps it was of no real consequence.

Solzhenitsyn is said to have thought that existence in the first place is primarily for the development of the Soul but on the other hand, Bernard would probably not have altogether agreed with him. Despite our basic

Catholicism he and I had only rarely debated religion in depth. The last time was during the year before his death when he told me that as a teenager he had adopted a great faith in Darwinism for a number of years, after studying the impressive flight achievements of various birds of prey. More latterly he had opted more towards Intelligent Design when considering their undeniably inspiring magnificence and beauty. These properties he believed could only emerge directly from a Divine Being.

As a man with specific religious convictions, the absence of any tangible evidence of his death and testament to his life seemed to amount to an odd sense of business unfinished. His became a passing where finality was postponed and it simply hovered about us, balanced uneasily. It soon became an event that could not even be comfortably discussed for fear of causing offence.

At some stage between his dying and the cremation in Lusaka that the British Consul had advised was the wisest course of action, there must have been a post-mortem investigation which might even have revealed that the cause of death had been due to ventricular fibrillation. It would have been true to say that his heart had not been in a completely healthy state for several years, occasioning regular visits to the Harley Street specialist said to be the best in his field. But information did not materialise to enlighten any of us other than possibly the wife he was about to desert for the sake of love. She remained tight lipped which is probably not completely unnatural under the circumstances. So tight were her lips and so long was the silence that we began to murmur one to another that the situation was more than simply odd, it grew stranger by the day. It was to be more than two months before the memorial service was organised in the city of Edinburgh that this story began with.

Despite the paucity of information in the intervening weeks and probably as a response to the forlorn tribute I placed myself in a public online forum, a trickle of messages filtered through to me from those who had known Bernard in his youth, school friends and neighbours from the surrounding streets where we both grew up. And each one of these communications and exchanges brought comfort and helped to fill the silence and the void.

I was both surprised and appreciative to hear from his first girlfriend. They had been sixteen at the time of their relationship, an intense romantic liaison that greatly concerned our poor mother and undoubtedly Christine's parents also. She was a delightfully pretty girl and Bernard was so very proud of her, so keen to show her off, especially to me as I was seen by him at that time as sophisticated beyond belief. Living in my London basement flat and working in Murrays Cabaret Club in Soho I undoubtedly saw myself in a similar light. I remember meeting with them both to sip gin at the Coach & Horses on The Hill at Northfleet where none of the Sunday bar staff seemed unduly concerned by their obvious youth. At that time my brother was quite convinced that their futures were inextricably linked and that he and Christine would adore each other for all time. Although that did not happen and things did not quite work out as he had visualised, he never forgot her, and often in the years that followed, spoke of her with a great deal of affection, exhibiting a fondness that clearly irritated both the women he finally went on to marry.

Despite the fact that Bernard never knew his father well enough for him to become a properly defined role model, he was to grow to resemble him in a myriad of ways. He had the very same charm and charisma, the same generosity together with a similar disregard for truth and inherent weakness of will where attractive women were concerned. And it was to be these latter personality traits that got him into a number of tight spots at times and caused so much distress to those who loved him. Despite his many faults, throughout his very nearly sixty-nine years of life he was possibly loved, admired and respected rather more than he deserved, just as his father had been.

But back in the time of that first love affair with Christine he had not yet grown into his adult persona and was diffident and lacking in confidence with a social awkwardness that would take a decade or two to entirely disappear. And there were to be little corners always that never entirely shook off the restrictions of his upbringing.

The very last time we spoke together, it was his Last Love rather than his First that was under discussion, and that discussion was both intense and powerful. It was a love that obscured all reason because it consumed his every waking thought and disturbed his sleep with dreams of an enchanted future. For Luiza he would throw aside the comfortable life he had built in North West Scotland and go to live with her wherever she might choose including the village by the Amazon where she had grown up if that was her wish. He had already undoubtedly thrown aside the regular visits to the Harley Street specialist in his desire to spend every precious London moment by her side. He would learn to speak Portuguese. He would buy a house for her family. He was rewriting his Will to include her, to ensure the security of his son, to accommodate the devastation of the impending matrimonial carnage. And within all this confusion his wife of thirty years was to be unceremoniously thrown aside because although his fondness and concern for her had not completely disappeared, it had become unseated by an infinitely greater passion over which he had no control whatsoever.

Distressingly for me he was to die before he could achieve many of the schemes and intentions he acquainted me with that night in the bar of his London hotel when I advised caution and he repeatedly told me that he needed me to be On His Side. But it was perhaps a fortuitous death as far as the wife who still loved him was concerned and although the silence that followed it was palpable it was understandable because the relinquishing of a partner through betrayal is not easy. The fact that his death then went oddly unobserved ensured that the memory of him would forever remain within the ranks of the detached and adrift. Nevertheless, for a few of us his presence lingers sharply etched and if I close my eyes I can hear his voice as clearly as if he was by my side as he once again embarks upon an entertaining tale that might well be completely true, but then again might not!

## About the Author

Jean Hendy-Harris is a free-lance writer who was born in England and lives in New Zealand. She developed a keen interest in writing as a child but when leaving school at fifteen decided to try life as a nun for a short period before being shunted into nursing. That didn't last long either and she soon found herself doing the shorthand and typing she had been trained for. Later she worked as a night club hostess for a number of years before moving to New Zealand with her young son and marrying an Auckland doctor. She home schooled two of her children for ten years and also ran a service providing school holiday seminars for gifted children.

Over the years she has been a short story writer for magazines and contributed articles on a regular basis on health and education to a variety of industry focused journals. She has three adult children and now lives in Auckland.

## OTHER BOOKS BY JEAN HENDY-HARRIS

`Chalk Pits and Cherry Stones' is a tale of childhood poverty and deprivation that would barely be recognised today, of food rationing and shortages, air raid warnings and Doodlebugs, overcrowding and neediness, a memoir of a time that is now almost forgotten.

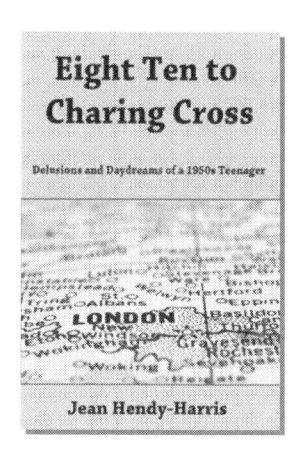

In the second part of her memoir Jean continues her story as a teenager in the 1950s. Yearning to escape the confines of her working class family and a mundane future as an office worker via a fast track to fame and fortune, she settles for the reflected glory of typing for the rising stars of popular music. Meanwhile her rich fantasy life becomes ever more elaborate.

**IN DISGRACE WITH FORTUNE**
*A Chronicle of Harlotry*
JEAN HENDY-HARRIS

All thoughts of Holy Orders, nursing and office work have finally been abandoned in this book as Jean applies for a job as a showgirl at a London night club. Later, after a drama-filled affair, she applies for a job with Madam Connie who runs a smart business in Belgravia catering to a wide range of sexual deviants. She also takes occasional typing jobs with Harley Street specialists and in her spare time begins to write articles and short stories for magazines.

Printed by Amazon Italia Logistica S.r.l.
Torrazza Piemonte (TO), Italy